T0129671

RIPPLES

in

TIME

Laurie Johnson

WESTBOW
P R E S S®
A DIVISION OF THOMAS NELSON
& ZONDERVAN

WestBow Press books may be ordered through booksellers or by contacting:

WestBow Press
A Division of Thomas Nelson & Zondervan
1663 Liberty Drive
Bloomington, IN 47403
www.westbowpress.com
844-714-3454

ISBN: 978-1-6642-9297-0 (sc)
ISBN: 978-1-6642-9298-7 (hc)
ISBN: 978-1-6642-9296-3 (e)

Library of Congress Control Number: 2023903001

Print information available on the last page.

WestBow Press rev. date: 07/11/2023

Contents

Time

I once sat down and counted my years,
surprised to find that I had less time to live
from this point in my life.
Much less time than I had spent living up to now.
Suddenly, I felt like a child who had won a packet of sweets
and eaten the first with pleasure.
But then realized that there were very few left.
Then I began to enjoy them intensely, taking
time to savor each flavor available, every second
counting for the tasting of these treats—
all that I could taste.
Watching the pieces getting fewer and fewer, with each bite.
I realized that I no longer have time for endless meetings,
meaningless relationships, unnecessary drama, or
statutes, rules, procedures, or eternal regulations,
where unrealities are the only things discussed.
I look ahead now, knowing that nothing will be achieved
by just talking about it or making future plans.
I realize now,
that I no longer have the time to support
the absurd, immature people who,
despite their chronological age, have not
grown up nor ever intended to
or who have no dreams, goals, or things they want
to accomplish, or enjoy in their short lives
My time is too short.
I know this now.
I desire the essence, the deepest understanding.
Now that my soul is in a hurry, I do not have many sweets left
in this almost-empty package anymore.
I realized that wasted time is like water poured into sand.
Once it's poured out, it can never be recovered again.

I want to live next to humble people,
very human,
those who know how to laugh at their mistakes,
those who are not inflated by their egos, those who
take on their responsibilities yet aren't afraid to live.
Thus, human dignity is defended, and we
move toward truth and honesty.
It is these essential things that make life worth living,
as I realize that life will go on.
I want to surround myself with people who know how to touch
hearts, people who have been taught by the hard blows of life
how to grow within
encouraged by gentle nudges
of the soul.
Yes, I am in a hurry. I am in a hurry to live with the intensity
that only maturity can give.
I don't intend to waste any of these leftover sweets.
I am sure they will be delicious,
much more than what I've eaten so far.
I just need the patience to take my time and slow down.
My goal is to reach the end satisfied and at peace
with my loved ones and my own conscience.
We have two lives, and the second begins
when we realize we have only one.
That is when we truly begin to live.

Laurie 2022

Standing On His Promise

I realized this morning I was barefoot.
I am not even sure that I own the right shoes
to walk the road, that lies ahead of me today.
I look ahead, and all I see are rocks with jagged edges, rough
spots, and deeper waters.
Missing boards on the wooded bridges
over huge ravines,
ones that I may not be able to cross.
Not on my own.
No, it does not make me doubt him.
I was just checking in for the day,
as I need to know what I should do,
how to traverse this road ahead.
I need to walk, sometimes run, but most days
I will do well to crawl.
Even when I doubt or wonder,
I know I can make it through it all.
I know by now that I have never yet been forsaken
or left alone,
and I know I never will.
But, Lord, how do I get over the questions
in my mind on those tough days?
Sometimes I'm so confused and plain scared.
It's like I am barefoot on a rocky path, and I
am scared to death of tripping again.
And on days like today, when it seems too much for me
to understand, I know the words written on my heart,
the teachings in my youth, and all the promises
you gave to me—all seven promises.
I will always remember them, and I will have no fear.
"In the days to come,
I will be with you.

I will protect you.
I will be your strength.
I will answer you.
I will provide for you.
I will give you peace.
I will always love you."
I whisper softly,
"Thank you, Lord," as I walk, and I continue to stand.
I stand on your promises.
This road ahead looks less threatening to me.
When I know, you're holding me closer.
I know when I fall,
even when I fall,
you never let me go.
I will rest, get back up again, and still be able to
move forward as I feel you gently take my hand
as I rise to start my day.

Laurie 2022

If You Ever Have a Daughter

If you should have a daughter instead of a son,
call her "Your Heart." The reason, you ask?
It is for all those hard days.
Those days, she will know that no matter what may come
her way, she can always find her way back to you.
That is what matters.
Then I am going to pray that God paints the solar systems
into the back of her mind
so, she will learn the entire universe
before she can say,
"Oh, I know that like the back of my hand."
And yes, she is going to learn that this life will hit her hard
in the face, and she will wait to get back up again,
just so it can knock her back down again.
But getting the wind knocked out of her sails
is the only way to remind her
that she can win, and she will again and again.
Yes, there will be hurt, the kind of hurts that cannot be fixed by
Band-Aids and Chocolate.
And then for the first time, she will
realize that help isn't coming.
She will have to stand on her own.
I will be sure and pray she knows.
She does not have to walk that lonely road alone.
She will never truly be by herself.
You will always remind her. God will always be there.
Always. Forever and a day.
Because no matter how far she roams or
how far she stretches those wings.
Trust me, those wings she will stretch too far at times,
and no matter what she does,
she will have to reach to attain those dreams,

sometimes dreams only she can see in her mind.
Where she is going or who she will grow to be someday
will be up to her.
Mama's hands will always be there to catch her when she falls.
All the hurts you will want to heal,
some will be harder to understand
as she grows so fast and will travel far.
Believe me, I've tried with my own each and every day.
But you will tell her,
"Baby girl,
please don't keep your head so high in the air like that.
I know that pose.
I've done it a million times myself.
You're just smelling smoke, so you can follow the trail back
to a burning house only to find that one
who lost everything in the fire,
just to see if you can save him or else find the one
who lit the fire in the first place,
just to see if you can change him."
But we all know no matter what you say, she will do it anyway.
So instead,
you can always keep an extra supply
of chocolate and rain boots
nearby, because there is no heartache that
your love and chocolate cannot fix.
OK, there are a few heartbreaks that chocolate can't fix,
but that's what the rain boots are for
because rain will wash away everything, making it like new.
All the heartaches, if she lets them,
combined with the time,
will all be well.
I want her to look at the world,
as if through the underside of a glass-bottom boat,
to look as if through a telescope at the galaxies that exist,
in the farthest imaginable places of a human mind,

because that's the way my parents taught me.
Just remind her,
"Remember your mama and papa are warriors."
Remind her that there will be days like this.
"There will be days," my grandma said,
"When you open your hands to catch the wind
but wind up with only blisters and
bruises or maybe a busted lip.
Or when you will step out of the plane and try to fly,
and the very people you wanted to help
are the ones still holding your parachute
with a smile and a wave.
Or when your boots will fill with rain and
you will be up to your knees with heartache
caused by the ones you wanted to save."
Those are the very days you have.
All the more reason to say thank you,
because there's nothing more beautiful
than the way the ocean refuses to stop kissing the beach
as it rolls onto the distant shorelines again and again.
It will never matter how many times,
how many years,
or how many storms
may have already been sent away.
She will put the wind in some of the victories,
probably lose battles more often than not.
She will put the star in, starting over and over.
That is the advice I would give.
And no matter how many times life erupts into a minute,
be sure her mind lands on the beauty of this crazy race
we call life.
And yes, on a scale from one to over
trusting, I am pretty darn naive.
But I want her to know, that this world is made like sugar.
It can crumble so easily,

but she should never be afraid to stick her hand out
and try to touch it,
to taste the very essence of life.
To step out and to live is to be all that she's afraid to be.
"Baby Girl,
I'll tell her to remember her family is a warrior family
and her papa will always be the hero
in Her eyes.
But you are the girl with small hands
and a huge heart and those
bright blue sparkling eyes.
The girl with that infectious smile that will
capture even the hardest of hearts."
That beautiful baby girl, who will never stop asking why
Looking for more adventure, more life, more
excitement, more time, more sunshine.
Remember that good things come in threes.
And so will bad things.
Teach her to always apologize
when she's done something wrong,
but never ask her to apologize,
for the way, her eyes refuse to stop shining,
how they light up a room when she walks in
and catches someone
else's eye.
How she changes a life with just a sweet smile
or questions, about their day.
Her voice is small, but it can change the world.
Don't ever let her stop singing or asking about the new things
that she sees.
And when life finally hands her heartache.
When it slips tears and pain under her door,
maybe even offers her an easy way out.
Make sure she will be able to tell that heartache,
that random thought,

even in that moment of despair
that they really ought to meet her God.
And that kind of fate
doesn't have a chance in her mind.
That would be my humble advice,
if you ever have a daughter.

Laurie 2022
Dedicated to little Miss Cora LeeAnn

A Lifetimes past

Shadows play in my mind.
Haunted memories of life.
Did I miss it, have I waited too long?
I see the shadows there, almost the same as yesterday.
As when I was young.
Those eyes, that smile,
that still haunts me.
With the same unanswered questions,
that I have seen so many years ago,
looking back at me.
In the reflection,
of this mirror of time.

Laurie 2022

Again

You will lose them over and over,
every minute of each and every day,
sometimes over and over in the same day.
So many different ways.
When the loss, momentarily forgotten,
you will begin to breathe again,
never really knowing when it will creep up.
And it will break your heart all over again.
Fresh waves of grief and lost love
as the realization hits home.
All over again as you forget and you call their name,
forgetting that they are gone, yet again.
You do not just lose someone and then you recover.
You lose them every time you open your eyes to a new day.
For as you awaken, so do your memories.
The forgotten bits of humor, little silly jokes.
Small memories.
As that the cleaving bolt of lightning rips into your heart,
as you remember they are gone again.
Losing someone is a lonely journey,
not a one off and a recovery in a day,
a week or a month.
There is no end to that loss.
There is only one skill learned.
That is how to keep your head above water.
As the waves hit you, like waves of the ocean.
As it comes crashing over the break wall, on to the sands.
So always be kind to those, who are sailing that stormy sea.
They have a long journey ahead of them
and a daily shock to their heart each time they realize.
Their loved ones are gone again.
You don't just lose someone once,

you lose them every day for the rest of your life.
It's not a journey we can take alone.
It's nice to have a friend just to talk to
when you need that extra nudge.
Each time we realize,
they are gone again.

Laurie 2022

An Angel

I often wonder if people ever know when
to them, an Angel may fly.
Do they know the day before or is this just a mystery?
As I look back to the time of loved ones,
I remember they are free from all the worries and care
of this crazy world.
I recall the stories and the memories of times past.
That are recited so well.
Until that day
you could no longer make a call to a mother,
just to say I love you.
That call to tell Dad how much you miss him.
A son who didn't make it home,
as if he knew
and the daughter in a hurry to call her mom.
Did she know that would be her last talk?
Are we given one last chance to sit quietly?
With that special one, or to just say hello,
is there an invitation to come home?
I think about this, and it must be true.
There must be so many angels
waiting and ready to go in a moment's notice
to fly down and bring us home.
Will we know?
When will an Angel come?

Laurie 2022.

In The Freedom of My Wings

As a bird locked up in a cage,
you called it love, as you turned the key.
Even as you clipped my wings.
Though you knew I was born to fly.
You said, oh pretty bird,
You cannot sing,
but I'll buy you treasures and shiny things.
Stay with me forever and a day,
like a bird locked up in a cage.
You knew I dreamed of how I would escape this place.
Of how I can fly higher and higher.
But how can I avoid the flames?
This fire goes higher and higher
and oh, I fear the flames,
yet you can't hold me down, forever.
No.
So, watch me now, as I dream.
Watch me as I fly away.
If only.
But in a dream.
I'm tired again and lost inside my mind,
all the twists and turns causing into chaos, within my heart.
You're twisted words are getting too sharp,
cutting deep into my thoughts.
As I say, no more wasted time.
See our stars?
They are no longer aligned.
Please, no more bruises.
No more battle scars.
I feel like a bird, locked up in a cage.
Oh, how can I escape this place?
And as I fly higher and higher.

Can I avoid these flames?
You can't hold me down anymore.
You can't pull me down, as I begin to soar.
So let me go.
Please release me.
Just let me fly away.
Even if it's but a dream.
To a day, when I'm no longer a prisoner.
When my heart has grown wings.
I'll show you what I'm worth.
I'm taking back what I deserve.
Release me, to be chained no more.
Take away the hurt and let me clear my mind.
As I fly away.
I am praying the Lord will give me a little faith,
as I struggle to escape this place.
I dream that I can fly higher and higher.
I fly above to avoid the flames,
as I fly through the fire.
The higher and higher I go.
Oh, you could not hold me down,
I just didn't know.
Oh, but you can't stop me now.
Can you hear me sing?
Are you listening?
As I fly free,
See me as I fly,
in the freedom of my wings.

Laurie 2022

To Live and Let Live

As I sat quietly on the mountains,
higher on the cliffs,
surrounded by a world of tumbling boulders and tumbleweeds,
I watched that natural grace and proud, noble walk.
As I see Mustangs, walk into sight, making their way
across the valley.
Hesitatingly, they approached the place where I'm sitting
an Oh,
for a brief moment in time, I see.
As one mare put her head down, we are eye to eye.
Face to face, spirit to spirit, her eyes speaking her story.
The echo of the wild Heart beating,
so wildly in her chest.
I sit here in awe, humbled to be in her shadow,
speaking my mind softly.
I hope you live here forever, until you take your last breath.
You are a majestic spirit.
Your hoof beats and your heartbeat will be heard,
echoing as a song.
Within the history of this mountain,
I breathed this out, as a simple prayer.
In these quiet moments,
alone in the wide-open spaces
beneath the crystal blue sky.
There is a peace and a sorrow that overwhelms my soul.
I know the depth and the heartache they will soon face.
I know the truth of what is happening.
They were born into this world, living in wild freedom,
born into their rightful place.
But all will soon be destroyed, and the people will take
what isn't theirs to take.
They will force their will upon these wild ones.

They will destroy this true and the wild spirit,
living as if it was a band of light running parallel
with the mountains,
into the open sky.
I pray for them as I pray for this nation,
for us to recognize
what we are losing, before it's too late.
Animals that are wild and sacred
as a way of life, they are tied to this land.
I'm praying for us to wake up,
stop managing parts of life,
that aren't in need of managing.
Even as we have regressed as a nation,
destroying living and wild beings.
Taking them from their rightful homes,
doing all that we can and dismantling their truth,
as they know it.
The crisis of our time
is that our minds have been manipulated
and our ideas formed
to give power to a dream or to an illusion.
As a whole, we have shifted to measuring growth
not in the terms of how life is enriched,
but in terms of how life should be lived.
Not on seeing,
how it will be destroyed
with the changes made.
All to make changes in the name of progress.
Whether it goes from bad to worse, never makes a difference.
I don't know the answer to all the questions.
No more than you will.
But will we ever stop and listen?
Our world doesn't need help to progress.
We just need to step back and let it go.
It was created to sustain and thrive

before we were ever created.
What do we think?
That we are so wise,
we know how to make it better?
Can't we just live and let live?

Laurie 2022

This Moment in Time

As I watched the vivid hues of a fading sunset dipping
below the horizon.
My heart smiles, in quiet contentment.
My heart is full, and my soul is no longer at war with the world.
As it bathes in the quiet peacefulness of the night,
the soft lull of the waves rolling softly over the sand,
creating ripples
as the memories do the same
in the back of my mind.
It's just one more reminder of the beauty and the moments
we can collect,
as I do the stones
walking along the Lake Shore.
As I stand, leaning my head back, with a deep breath,
I close my eyes and in that moment,
I can feel the serenity of the quiet evening
as it settles over me like a warm and cozy blanket.
This very moment is the reason why.
The very reason,
I stopped looking for the next thing to buy,
the next place to go and the next person to make me happy.
None of which ever really made me feel alive
or even passionate,
as if I had ever had a true purpose in my life.
I thought having all the latest and the greatest
would fill the empty places in my heart and life.
But it never did.
I kept going from one place to the next,
thinking I'd find what I was looking for,
what I was missing in my life.
Never realizing,
I was looking in all the wrong places

for all the wrong things.
Until I stopped one day and started listening to my own heart.
I stopped chasing the moments,
the adventures,
new places,
that I thought would make me want to come alive.
I have been wishing for something or someone.
Now I realize it would never have happened anywhere
that I had been looking.
But now, being present in my life,
living in the moment,
putting away my phone and appreciating the beauty,
in the quiet moments of life.
That has changed everything about me
and what I thought
I wanted to find.
I want to do all the things the world.
Seems to have forgotten about.
Lying in the sand, under a star filled sky.
As off on the horizon, seeing the glow of the Northern Lights
as they ribbon across the midnight skies.
Turning down the noise of life and turning up the music,
feeling the wind in my hair and grasping at forever.
As time
passes through my hands.
That last song, the last first kiss,
the last bite of a chocolate bar.
Those are the moments, I'll spend my life doing,
all the while seeking for the contentment
of just this moment.
Sure, tomorrow will still be there, and
reality will always intrude.
It's always right there around the corner.
I know that life will still be in motion, like a ship setting sail.
But today, right now, in this moment,

I want to immerse myself in these immeasurable experiences
that free my mind and electrify my spirit.
In these moments, I could live forever.
Lost in this moment of time.

Laurie, 2022

In Time

As she sits in the quiet of the shadows of the night.
She realizes that she's truly alone.
She the one,
who has always been there to catch each and everyone
as they fell.
She, who had always been ready to fill the void
for all
who had needed that extra space and time.
Or to take up the weight, from their shoulders,
willing to carry the load, for a spell.
But now, no one had any idea, what to do for her.
There is no one there.
All the years of past support and the people now gone.
The ones that she is helped and the ones she stood by,
who will be there when she needs someone?
When she needs someone to stand in that space,
between her and the void consuming her mind.
And in that void of need.
Who will step forward,
in time?

Laurie, 2022

Understanding

Being in a relationship with a hard working
independent man or woman
is not for everyone.
That is why some people these days, are interested
in the partners with no life perspective.
The thing to understand is.
That he or she, might not always be
available for you.
You may think there are times
when they will not seem to be invested
in the relationship.
But it's not the case at all.
It's actually quite the opposite, in fact.
They wake up every morning
and work hard every chance
they can,
trying to create a stable present
or future for themselves and you.
If you choose to do that, you need to understand
there will always be days
when they will most likely be tired
and will barely have time to take a shower.
As they give you a kiss before heading to bed
for some much-needed rest.
Just to start all over again, the first thing the next morning.
Do not take this kind of person for granted.
Believe me, they are hard to find.
They might come off a little rough around the edges
because of dirty calloused hands and a greased stained shirt.
Possibly tired from being on their feet for 16-18 hours a day,
but this individual will love you.
They will love you with the type of love

you have never experienced before,
with the same intensity, in which they live their life.
So here is to the hard-working people
that are married to the partner of their dreams,
that get up every morning and work hard every day
for their families to be able to live a life
of which they have always dreamed.

Laurie, 2022

Dear Me

It's okay to feel a little overwhelmed and confused at times.
It's okay to feel a little lost and uncertain about life
in general, some days.
It's okay to feel a little uneasy,
about some things.
Just listen to your heart.
Also, it's okay to occasionally feel like your worthless,
discouraged or even disheartened with everyday life.
Just don't stay there too long.
There will be times in your life
when you are filled with questions,
to which you have no right answers.
And times when you are filled with answers
to yet unspoken questions.
Times when life is smooth, easy sailing as it can get.
The wind is right, water is perfect, and the sun is shining bright.
And other times when it will be a bumpy ride.
Unpredictable winds, clouds that cover any light
you could have seen.
Times when things are messy all over the place,
utter chaos will reign
and life is completely out of hand.
But other times when things are clear, comprehensible,
and all just goes as planned,
so much easier to understand.
Sometimes when we take time
for a bit of soul searching.
That's when we might question where we are meant to go.
Where are we meant to be?
Or if we even know what we are meant to do
or who we are meant to meet?
Life will involve a lifetime of adventures

to be either relished in
or to be simply endured.
Roads to be traveled,
paths to be walked, waters to be navigated,
all new experiences and endeavors.
It will be our choice to make.
You are always traveling
in so many different directions
and what works for one person,
may not work for you.
What is best for one person
may not be the best for you.
Understand,
that there will always be different circumstances.
Difficult situations and odd occurrences,
that they are all completely out of your control,
you will have to trust in God's plan.
It will create moments of disappointment,
pain and frustration,
sometimes even fear and chaos in your life
for you to overcome.
But you have no need to beat yourself up
when things don't unfold, the way you expected them too.
Maybe they're not how you expected them to be.
But things will always work out,
just give it time and a quick prayer.
There are times when it will be necessary
for you to guard your
Peace of Mind.
To withdraw yourself temporarily from your surroundings
and reconnect with yourself.
Your own feelings, your heart, and your purpose
to regain your courage, clarity
and self-confidence, along with some peace of mind.
Learn your own strengths

with the ability to use them.
But during these hard times,
I hope you simply refuse to remain trapped
in a place of confusion
and heartache.
Not feeling at home
or the feeling of not being wanted there.
I hope you believe in the possibilities that lie ahead,
because they are endless.
And I hope you trust in that, one day.
You will reach a point in time trusting your own perspective
and will be standing tall.
When you have learned to celebrate
your own special uniqueness,
complete differences and utter authenticity.
As others will come to accept you
in those unique ways.
When you can see the bigger picture,
celebrating where you are going,
of how you are growing.
Only then, will you understand these words.
You will understand.
That while times of struggle,
heartache and difficulty,
which unfortunately will be inevitable.
Trust that things will fall into place,
that the tough times won't last forever.
Each and every morning is a brand-new beginning.
On which the sun will shine again,
on yet another day.

Laurie 2022

Remember

To always stand tall beneath the morning sun,
greet the day with your smile.
Remember life's not always perfect.
Good things take a while, sometimes even a lifetime.
Remember to always give thanks
for the small ways
in which you've been blessed.
For the love you have been given,
for the heart that still beating within your chest.
Ask not for what you want,
but for the things that you can do.
Think of those less fortunate,
before you think of you.
And don't forget to listen to the birds that sing up high.
Don't forget the simple joys
like the clouds, hovering in the sky.
Enjoy the sun that warms you
as it shines down on your face.
And don't forget to smell the roses along the way,
even in your hurried day.
And as you rush about,
remember what's important still,
you simply can't take a life and bend it to your will.
And now, before I go,
one more memory yet to come.
Don't forget to look around giving thanks
for all you see.
Stop and smell the roses,
to watch the flowers as they grow.
Be happy with your place in this life.
Be humble to your neighbors and never forget to say hello.
Don't take even a moment of your life for granted.

Or of all the things you feel and see.
For you have but one life to live.
For in this moment in time,
you have but a moment to give.
Always remember
Sincerely, your heart.

Laurie, 2022

Did You Know?

Someone out there somewhere is thinking of you.
Did you know?
Someone out there is replaying the soft lilt of your voice,
the way you turn your head, as you speak.
Replaying in their head, the words you had spoken
Maybe they are replaying your words,
over and over in their mind.
To help them make a difficult decision or just make it
through a hard day.
Someone, somewhere is missing that hidden side of you
that only they had known.
Did you know?
Someone, somewhere is whispering your name,
wishing they had asked that question so long ago?
Did you know?
That someone, somewhere is speaking of you.
As you read these words, praising your soft
heart and all the little things that you do?
Someone somewhere
is replaying all the memories in their lives.
That was only of you.
That way you made them feel as if they were
important and needed. That was you.
Did you know someone, somewhere is missing your smile?
Remembering, how it once lit up the room, when you walked in.
Realizing now that light can only be found
when they see that smile upon your face.
When they watched you, watching as
it would light up that sparkle
so brightly in your eyes.
Do you know that someone somewhere
is wishing for more time?

Wishing they had taken the time to sit down with you.
And laugh and talk over the little things you say and do.
Someone, somewhere is missing your love.
The way you made them feel, as if no one
else in the world mattered as much
as they mattered to you,
in that moment, long ago.
That was you.
Did you know?
That someone, somewhere is thinking of you.
about all the little silly thing,
that are what makes up that special person that you are?
Did you know?
That someone somewhere, once felt so very lost?
At their wits end,
looking for a reason to go on, in the speed
and the chaos of this life?
It had come at such an unexpected cost.
They had given up.
Until you came along, with that smile
and you showed them their worth.
That was you.
Did you know?
That treasure that someone is thinking of.
That is you.
Did you know?

Laurie 2022

Who You Were Meant to Be

Do you ever wonder why
we stay in a certain place,
when we don't even fit in?
Maybe because we were taught to believe,
there is no place, that would be any different.
That would embrace all that we are?
We bind ourselves up, trying to fit into a mold
where we were never meant to be.
But that will only work for just a short while.
You're living in a dream world,
where you're told to live a fantasy
that will never be a reality.
So, we go along and convince ourselves,
our wild weirdness and our dreams are just too much.
Our bold voices, too inappropriate.
Our way of blunt honesty,
is just too much for most to handle.
We learned to draw away and hide within ourselves,
being told, not to cause offense,
with our way of speaking or our mannerisms.
We are finally convinced that we would never fit
into anyone else's world.
Never to be accepted.
We are just too different.
we convince ourselves that we should keep hidden
the true essence
of whom we really are.
We hide behind the facade of a quiet, private person.
In this world we live in, where we have
grown, on a diet of being different,
of never being enough.
Why would we ever think otherwise?

We feel the pressure of it as soon as we think about it,
that passion to fit in and be like everyone else.
This soul deep crushing, sinking, venomous feeling
as we dance within our own uniqueness.
It feels toxic because it is.
It's not true.
But sadly, that is the way of life.
It's a cruel and slow way to die.
It's a lie, and it always has been.
Always will be.
Being difficult or different is not a sin.
It's a blessing in disguise.
You are different, but that doesn't make
you unworthy or difficult.
You are more than enough and always were,
always will be your voice.
You were meant to be heard,
your imagination was meant to be seen,
and your dreams were meant to take flight.
Stand up and be proud of who you are, proud of yourself,
of whom you have become.
Being too much, in a world
that has too little.
You are told, you love too hard.
Like there will never be enough love.
Dance wildly, as if no one is watching.
Staring at the moon as it fades away, into a brilliant sunrise.
Thinking of all the possibilities.
Go ahead and dig down deep.
Take these chances.
Be heard and be seen.
Do all the incredible things that make you,
Who you are.
Because each time you decide to be you
You shed more of the disguise,

You were taught to cover your uniqueness,
hiding that person, you truly are.
The more uncovered and honest you are,
the more of you can be seen
by the ones who you are meant to meet.
Just because you don't fit into a mold,
just because you are different,
doesn't mean you have failed.
It means you grew past the box and now the time
has come to break free to be who you were.
Always meant to be.

Laurie 2022

Enough

I'll always be too much for some.
I'm finally realizing that
that's okay.
To be too much for those that think that,
just as it's okay to be
not enough for others
that expect the impossible
or demand a change,
I get excited over simple, silly little things,
sometimes even over the
oddest little something
that may mean nothing to someone else.
Some of which I'm sure
will make absolutely no sense to you.
I get emotional over weird things
that most would never even care about,
or even take the time to try and understand.
Almost everything with family has a sentimental value to me.
Which means I have a hard time letting go of some things.
At times, clutter and chaos will stress me out.
Yet other times, I can thrive in the chaos and ignore the clutter.
I talk too much at times, but maybe not enough at other times.
Some days my thoughts are too loud.
My brain is always like a web browser
with three hundred different tabs opening, all at once.
Still trying to open more?
Maybe to see why turnips are purple or if Penguins have knees.
Who knows?
I might send multiple text messages when I
could have sent it all in one message.
Sometimes I type faster, than my thoughts flow.

Before they can even say go, I am off
and running in a new direction.
I give my all on anything I do.
More often than not, I laugh at myself more than anyone else.
I love corny jokes at times.
Other times not so much.
I sing the most random songs at the top of my lungs.
I will always be that wild child deep down inside,
always young at heart.
I crave simplicity,
Yet at the same time, I am always dreaming of bigger things.
I'm basically a toddler in a little Tykes car,
going one hundred miles an hour,
in a twenty-five mile per hour speed zone.
When I start watching a show or series,
I must finish it all at once.
I can't stand not knowing how it will end.
When I write a song, I play it over and repeatedly
till I can sing it without hesitation.
I love it when songs are written and speak to me.
I love it when lyrics or quotes relate or make me stop and think.
Makes me feel, what they were feeling,
as they wrote these words.
Living with these emotions, experiencing life in a completely,
Or a unique and different way,
almost as if I'm in their world,
If only for that day.
I have a hard time saying no to anyone needing help,
even if there is already too much on my plate.
I'm always trying to learn new things, new hobbies, new crafts.
I change my mind a lot in many random ways.
I changed directions and started something new.
I live for a busy, chaotic, on-the-go lifestyle, yet at the same time
I want to stay home and be private.
I'm a crazy hermit who likes to be home alone,

working in my house or in my garden,
even spending half the day, just talking to the chickens or quail,
listening to what they might have to say in return.
I'm constantly worrying
if or why some people seem to dislike me.
But then I can meet someone else and
instantly become friends,
as if I have known them my entire life.
So, I have come to realize, it doesn't matter either way.
Sometimes I sleep too much, but most nights
I don't sleep at all, never a happy medium
or a balance to that state of mind
Simply because my brain won't stop rewinding
around and around, through every scenario in my mind.
But you know what I am?
I am loyal to a fault and will always defend my people
without ever thinking twice.
Nothing makes my day brighter
than making someone else's day better.
I give my all in everything that I do.
I dream hard, but I work even harder.
I do fall hard when I trip and go down, but I get back up
and I try over and over again.
Quit, is simply not a word in my vocabulary.
When I love, I love unconditionally, but I trust completely also
which is my greatest fault.
I may love too much. I may always laugh too much.
I may sing too much. I know, I feel too much.
When it comes to emotions, I always forgive too much.
I am too much.
I know this for a fact, but I will no longer apologize
for being this way.
I have come to realize, that I will never be everyone's cup of tea,
For my glass is always half full, versus half empty,
That is just the way I choose, to see my life.

I am not perfect, but I like who I am becoming.
A person that I can be proud of.
I don't have it all figured out yet, but in time I will.
I don't have all that I want,
but I always have all that I need, whatever it is for.
That is how my life seems to be for me.
And that is enough,
for whom I have chosen to be.

Laurie 2022

My Way to Fly

Everyone tells me that I should lower my expectations
and be more realistic, in my way of life.
That I can't possibly finish,
all that I have started
That I need to stop believing
in my unrealistic dreams and my stance.
The truth is, I'm never going to listen to all the people.
Telling me what I can and cannot do,
or even what I should or shouldn't want
or how I should or shouldn't live.
They have never had to walk in my shoes.
Nor could they ever understand my reasons.
Or why life has pushed me to go over and beyond
each and every day.
Maybe for them, ordinary and average is enough.
But I'll never be that "normal person" and I don't want to be.
Even if that's OK for them,
they can live and be content with a normal life.
To live their last days without passion,
pushing aside their dreams as foolish
and just doing
what everyone else thinks is normal.
If I'm doing something, loving someone, or chasing my dream,
I'm always going to be giving it my all.
There is no halfway for me,
I will walk away if I can't put all my heart and soul into
this life. There is no excuse for me to give in and relax.
Let someone else live my dreams.
This just who I am and who I always will be.
I know that I will have days when I get knocked down more
than I can stand back up,
and those times when life brings me to my knees,

I will always remember being told, to be knocked down
is not a failure, but failing to stand
is when I become a failure.
I will never stay down, and I will never quit.
I want so much more out of this life,
and I'll only get there if I keep going.
I intend to keep fighting and continuing to rise above,
even if I am following a dream, that no one else can see.
They may wonder, what I'm looking at or what I see
And that's okay.
I know it will not be easy and I will want to quit
some days more, than I'll want to fight,
but I'm still going to keep pressing forward.
There's so much more for me still to do,
and a lot of life, love, and joy to discover.
It's just waiting for me to show up and find it.
So, excuse me, while I pull my wings from the fire.
And I have learned how to fly stronger and higher
than I did yesterday.
I am still learning who I am.
I don't know where I'm headed
but there's a star out there, in that clear midnight sky
with my name on it.
And I do intend to see it,
for that's exactly why I'm headed upwards
farther every day.
This is my time and my choice.
And I'm making it all that it can be.
No matter how hard it gets or how wild that wind blows,
bringing the storms and driving rains
that always seems to find me.
I am meant for more, more than just an ordinary existence.
I've got this.
I always have had.
I just never knew it before, I had failed to see.

So that's what I'm fighting for.
More happiness, more Peace of Mind,
more love, more life to call my own.
More passion and more purpose.
I'll get there in time, just wait and see.
I might even find new wings, somewhere along the way.
But then,
You just never know, maybe then
I will have learned why,
I needed to fly.

Laurie 2022

Together, We Can

For as far back as I can remember,
I was everything for everyone,
the hub for the proverbial wheel that was our family.
As I got older,
I had come to the realization, they all depended on me
to be the one to solve everything and to be the strong one
who was supposed to overcome any challenge.
To come up with the solutions to equal things out
and make everyone happy, keep the balance, so to speak.
This is just who I was.
I was always supposed to be the strong one,
but no one ever seemed to remember that I was human too.
They all thought I was unbreakable,
unshakable, and unstoppable.
I was there to catch them when they fell if there was ever a fall.
A new baby born, or the one who
keeps the wolf from the door,
so, to speak.
And maybe that was true to a point,
but more than that,
I was expecting to be there, before all else.
But even I had a breaking point.
The problem was no one ever took the time to see that.
The time to notice,
I was the one faltering and spinning out of control.
So, there was no one to catch me when I fell
but even as I realized this, it was already too late for me
As I spiraled out of control, I had to finally admit,
I was on my way down.
It was then, I realized; I was truly on my own.
I had never taught anyone to take care of anyone else,
while I was taking care of them.

So, as I was spinning round and round, going from
problem to problem, saving everyone else,
I was drowning in those same storms and waves,
crashing against me, day after day.
The same waves, that I had helped anchor
everyone else against.
It was those very storms, which were taking me under
more and more with every crash,
battering me against the shore.
I was struggling, to stay afloat in the chaos,
but at the same time
I was fighting to help them through theirs, helping them stand,
making amends and meeting demands.
And truthfully, I was so utterly exhausted.
I had nothing left for my own little family, much less for myself.
I'm sure I'll find a way through all of this,
I would think, I just need some time to just think, then I'll rest.
I would say this over and over again,
never realizing that day would never come.
Never seeing that my own boys were growing up, without me
watching me take care of everyone else.
I know now that I needed to make the time, to step away,
to take care of my own, away from everyone else.
They would move forward without me.
That's a hard lesson to learn.
But I didn't get a choice in learning that lesson.
Life made that choice for me,
and I came to the cruel and instant halt
at the worst possible time in my life.
I lost it all in the blink of an eye.
Just a second though it seemed as if it
must have lasted an eternity,
or so it seemed to me.
A hard lesson learned that we are only human,
and there is only so much we can handle alone.

We are just not that strong.
In time, I may find that I get overwhelmed by life again
but now I know better.
I am stronger now.
I know when to stop now.
So, I'm stepping back every now and again, to catch my breath
and regain my strength, to find my purpose in life once again.
That doesn't mean I will stop being the resilient person
that tries to anchor everyone, in the wind
Or who they count on me, to be.
Only that I realize, now that I can't
keep my fire burning brightly
if I don't do things, that allow me to feed my own soul,
whether it's rest, reflection, or just time to recharge
a week of quiet or a month away,
I'm going to make the effort and take the time for myself
if I am to survive.
But I don't want to just survive, to just get by or just tread water
for the rest of my life.
I want to feel alive, and I want to do my best
and always, always be the best version of myself
that I can be now,
especially in everything I say or everything that I do.
So, excuse me if I disappear every so often, rekindle my energy.
As I collect my thoughts and try to make sense of life again,
for me, for you, and for everyone else,
I'll always be that strong person, capable of doing everything
and anything that I am able to do.
The difference is, from now on,
I won't be drowning myself, to be everyone else's anchor.
We can all sink or swim together.
Then together,
maybe we can continue to rise.

Laurie 2022

Just a Word of Advice

Go quietly into your day.
Even amid all the noise and hurried haste.
Always remember when in peace, there can be silence.
Never feel left out.
If you are left in peace, keep yourself as far away as possible
without surrender.
Be on good terms with all people.
Speak your truth quietly. Always be polite.
Speak softly and clearly.
Always listen to others, even the ones that others have dubbed
as dull and ignorant.
They too have their stories to tell.
Avoid loud and aggressive people
that are dangerous to a gentle soul.
Never compare yourself with others.
You will become vain and bitter,
for there will always be
greater and lesser people than yourself.
Enjoy your achievements and celebrate your victories
as well as your plans.
Stay interested in your own career, however humble.
It is a real accomplishment to be charged
With changing the fortunes of time,
Exercise caution in your business affairs,
for the world is full of trickery and new ideas.
Never let this blind you to what virtue
there is in the population of certain ones.
So many people will strive for higher ideals,
and everywhere life is full of heroism.
But be yourself, especially in your relationships.
Do not feign affection or expect it from shallow people.
Do not stand by the sidelines and wait to be noticed

until people are done,
with spending time with their family or friends.
Until they are gone, then you exist again.
When they're gone, never be cynical about love,
for in the face of all adversity and disenchantment,
It is as essential as the grass.
Take kindly and to heart the council of years of wisdom,
gracefully surrendering to the trappings of youth.
Nurture as strength of spirit to shield you,
when sudden misfortune strikes, or whenever the storms
may find you, even within a safe harbor.
Consider this.
Do not distress yourself with dark
things that could happen.
Not that has happened.
Many fears are born of fatigue and loneliness, insecurities,
or fears of failing beyond wholesome discipline.
Be gentle with yourself.
Don't be so hard or critical of each and every bump in your life.
You will be okay, adopt the motto
"It is, what it is."
You are a Child of the King, no less than the trees and the stars.
You have the right to be all that you can be.
And whether or not it is clear to you,
never doubt the plan is unfolding as it should.
Therefore, be at peace with God, as you conceive him to be,
and in whatever your labors
or aspirations are in this noisy confusion of life
Keep peace within your soul.
With all its shame and drudgery and broken dreams,
it is still and it can be a beautiful world.
Be cheerful, work to be happy.
Keep a smile and a voice of gratitude
in everything that you do.

Laurie 2022

Just a Talk

Have a seat.
A little coffee and a lot of talk.
Have a seat.
There's no reason to stand or walk about.
Let's talk about the things that are new.
Gossip like we're setting on the back pew,
exchanging stories of yesterday's adventures.
To tell of the things, as we know they went.
Another cup of coffee, as the tales continue to grow.
There is so much that only we know.
The couple that moved into the Old Brown farm.
They seem so nice.
They'll do no harm.
The other night the police raced by sure hope no one was hurt,
I said with a sigh.
This little town is the place to live,
many good people are not afraid to give.
Everyone knows what the neighbors are doing,
which is good when a stranger is a fooling.
Our talk has gone on for most of the day,
Oh my
We have had a lot to say.
These days are the best when sharing with a friend,
especially with a friendship that has no end.
We don't see each other every day, maybe not even in a week,
but that's OK for when we find time to speak,
We have so much to say
just to keep this moment in time.
Just a little bit longer.
One last cup before we part
there is always that chance that
we will start again.

Laurie 2022

Hearts

We all have different hearts
made out of many different things.
Some are carved out of pain, some are decorated
with rare gems, days of joy and laughter,
memories of times past.
Some hearts are open to everyone, fully trusting in all,
but some you need a key to enter
they may have taken a hard fall.
You find hearts that are made purely of flowers, that can
spread their petals, taking charm everywhere they go.
Then there are hearts that offer shade to those
who are weary
and just need a break.
Yet then again, some hearts will burn you without hesitation
when you try to get too close.
You may come across hearts that are filled with music,
some who bleed for the world who hurts.
Certain hearts have enough space
to let people inside all the time,
and yet some are closed to anyone who attempts to even try.
Some hearts are soft, others are ice cold.
Some are broken, missing to many parts to ever be whole.
There are hearts overflowing with memories
and others that live life so passionately
that they grab at it each moment together,
Adding more memories into their heart's.
We meet hearts that are torn, broken and bleeding.
Our hearts are tenderized by the repeated knocks of life.
Some hearts are sweet as candy, yet others bitter as gall.
No matter what type of heart you have
or what type of heart you get to deal with every day,
No matter who it belongs to,

a heart is still one of the most sacred things ever created
and out of all the different types of hearts we encounter
to me the most beautiful heart
is a grateful heart.

Laurie 2022

It Is, What It Is

Her journey has been a hurricane some days,
a tidal wave, a dark path of highs and lows,
so many battles with few victories.
She never wanted to be this fighter,
but it seems that life had other plans for her beautiful soul.
As every day, she steps out into this world of harsh reality.
Yet she is determined to be there and ready to tackle
anything life throws at her.
So, whatever may be coming her way
on any given day, she'll be the first to tell you
that she gets knocked down
more often than not, she fails more than she triumphs,
but she always gets back up and keeps fighting.
She will tell you she will never fail,
unless she refuses to get back up.
She's just not wired to quit.
Not in her life, not on the people that depend on her,
or on the dreams she wants to achieve.
Most times the dreams are ones
that only she can see.
She will simply say, it is, what it is.
Some marvel at her strength, thinking she's always been tough.
They have no idea the number of times
that she's been broken and somehow pulled away
To hide, as she put herself back together again.
Each time she came back stronger, wiser, and better.
The Japanese people have an ancient custom,
that she loves to think upon.
That custom is to repair a broken cup or plate with gold,
to fill in the cracks and hold it back together,
making it strong again.
That it is considered a great honor to use that broken dish.

Now that it has been repaired with gold,
It's now a precious, unique, and coveted treasure.
She has never lamented the broken hearts or the bad times,
the hard lessons learned.
It is what it is.
She's decided that she has learned and grown
from each experience they have made her into what
And who she is today.
That woman you see today, with a
seemingly indestructible spirit
and a heart of gold.
But she has paid dearly for everything she has done
and who she will become as time passes.
She wanted to give up, stay down and rest so many times,
but she knew she still had so much more to do
and many more days to live.
So, when you catch her smiling through the tears
or laughing through the pain and battling for her joy,
struggling to just simply stand
or when you see her struggle for balance.
Remember to appreciate her and all for which she is fighting.
She is an utterly unique creature.
Despite the odds sometimes stacked against her,
she will always manage to find her way,
finding a way to make it work.
That's because she has learned, what many have not.
She knows how to keep flying higher and higher
with a broken spirit.
There may be pain, but to her,
failure is not an option.
It just isn't in her vocabulary.
And no matter how hard life tries to bring her down,
She will not give that up.
And that's why she will always rise again.
She will stand again, and life will still happen.

It may mean some minor adjustments to her plan,
but it will get done.
And with a smile, she will simply say
It is, what it is.
And that's okay.

Laurie 2022

How To Kill a Butterfly?

When you see the storm behind her eyes,
you know, you will never understand her.
Will you still begin your world of lies?
You even act as though you're surprised, to have found
a kindred and wise soul,
as you hide behind your clever disguise.
She will never know......or so you surmise.
That you will expect her to change, to be as you want her to be.
All in due time, your time.
As your secrets begin to stretch so far and wide,
you keep expecting her to change.
For you will never accept her as she is
even as you look into her eyes, swearing you have.
A shattered past, she's trying to just stumble thru,
she pulls together, trusting you as she goes.
Yet you move forward as the truth belies, what you say.
You think she will change in time.
It just must be, as you say it will be, it's the only way.
When she has her doubts, you rush to assure her
you accept her as she is.
Because the alternative now,
would be to lose her.
And of that possibility, your terrified.
Yet, as she questions you,
you never realize she's counting the times carefully.
Watching as reality slips beneath your disguise,
she feels betrayed and hurt.
At times, she is even ready to fly.
You try to act quickly, before she has time to ask you why.
These questions you can't afford to answer.
Tell her you're not like the other guy,
as you give her your made-up alibis.

Then as she looks you straight in the eye,
you swear true love until you die.
Swearing that you would never leave
her, as had been done before.
But she's been hurt, and she is wise.
So, as she watches your eyes shutter to hide
the lie, she heart releases a sad sigh.
For she knows when she's hearing that line.
As she begins to modify her actions, in the way she replies,
carefully guarding each time.
Now you know you will need to pacify her, to calm her fears.
So, as you begin to see the storms moving,
swirling in the depths of her eyes,
you decide to steer against her.
You need to disqualify her fears, make them unimportant.
To make her believe you would never be dissatisfied.
That you are content as you pull her back in,
just before she has time to fly away.
You could trim her wings, but you hate to make her cry.
She needs to know all that you have sacrificed,
no matter how small, you make her feel.
She needs to know what it has cost
you, adding her into your life.
Above all, that is all that matters to you, how much it has cost.
You will never see how her heart is breaking and her
mind, is stupefied, as she begins to see her past repeat.
To realize her brain, it has misidentified your motives.
She believed you to be as honest,
as you had seemed at the start of this life.
This............. is how you kill a butterfly.
Drip fed slowly on a short supply of deliberate lies.
She held on to a fragile hope, that this time was true.
So, you start pouring out emotions
quickly, to intensify the effects.
Then take it back, don't over apply.

You need her to believe your lies, to believe you are content,
As content as she was, at the start.
You know to lose her now, would mean your demise.
Yet.... you are not satisfied, nor as content as she is.
You want more than she can give.
So, you give the ultimatums without pause.
It's a constant push requiring her to change, to comply.
You will never accept her as she is, that is just your way,
and your way is the only way.
She will come to realize this in time.
Yet she keeps that wall strong and built high.
You never stopped to realize; it was built to keep one like you
from hurting, what that wall hides inside.
Oh, and don't forget to keep hidden
your list of lies.
Remembering your excuses, your alibies.
Each time your demeanor slips and she catch glimpses
of what you hide.
Do not forget to multiply what she owes you
over and over each time.
Keep reminding her of how much you love her,
when she questions why?
Remind her, she owes you, when she catches that lie.
Be sure to keep the truth, cleverly hidden behind your lies.
You know she would be gone in an instant,
if she ever sees that side.
Yet losing patience, you must have your say.
Things will change or nothing, you must have your way,
things must change now.
She owes you that much, you repeat inside your mind.
Even though you know, she will walk away.
Then you just let her leave,
with no goodbyes or regrets at the time.
You're in the right, as you justify what is happening.
Taking apart her life, one brick at a time,

You are convinced, you deserve so much more
than she has to give.
So many have told you this, time after time.
You can find someone else who will do as you ask.
Who appreciates you in the ways,
you have been told,
it should be.
So, you let her go,
letting her believe, she has failed.
You'll watch her fly away.
Never giving her time
to realize the lies you have told to all around her.
Anyone who would listen, to tell them how she did you wrong,
how she owes you.
Oh no, you would rather die, if they thought you were to blame.
Then you see her again and intuitively know regret.
You realize she walked away, with all
that had ever mattered in your life.
All to let you find what you thought you were missing,
gone in the blink of an eye
She's not really telling anyone, anything?
But she would never lie, to hide the
reasons, behind her decision.
No one needed to know, her private life.
Yet never understanding,
why someone else would need to do that to her?
Or why would you keep her close, then just let her go.
While destroying all around her, when she was gone.
This........ is how you kill a butterfly.
Always.
Always keep that, in the back of your mind.
Why did you need to ask her to change?
Always, making sure to remind her
how much it has cost you.
How much you have given for her sake.

You need her, to need you.
So that you can continue to lie to yourself.
The truth is just, too hard to admit.
That you lost it all when she left your side?
That she had given all, that she had to give.
Maybe, now you will realize, but no.
You will tell the world your side, try to crucify her character
with more lies.
You keep your true motives disguised, your hurt pride.
You feel the need to keep playing the victim,
making sure you will never take the blame.
Making sure, no one would ever have time to realize.
She was the one, that had nothing to hide.
She had been honest from the start
about love
and how her life was.
She had given all she had, each and every day.
She had given all of herself, in so many small ways.
That was her way of taking care of the people, she cared for.
But she had watched the storms building, behind your eyes.
Watched you become, what she had already surmised.
She knew that there was always something dishonest,
behind your disguise.
You hid it well, but time had cracked your mask
and it showed in your eyes.
When she questioned you and you told
those first few white lies.
Even as you kept assuring her, all was well.
You were content as life was, you said.
This was enough.
Even then, she already knew.
You were not all that you claimed to be.
She had accepted that, knowing
that you expected more than she had to give,
yet trusting in your words.

knowing that you were a broken lullaby
to which she could never quite finish, a melody too.
She tried so hard to justify you actions, to convince herself.
Always trying to make it OK.
That life would be good, that she would be enough this time,
but the love she gave, realizing it would
never be enough even now.
The little things, she put into each and every day,
she realized, would never have been enough for you,
as the lies were magnified.
And as time passed, she knew the score.
But with you she had dropped her disguise.
She had let that guard down, the one that had kept her safe
inside that wall,
the one that held her hurt and kept the pain away.
But for her, you couldn't even try.
It had to be more.
There would be no compromise.
There were others out there, you said you could find.
You had your head filled with the wisdom of others' advice.
They didn't care if you lost at all.
They just couldn't stand having her that close.
They would rather you be alone to cater to their whims
than to have someone else in your life, besides them.
So, the more you listened, the more disgruntled you became.
The more you wanted from her,
more each and every day.
Until it had built into a mountain, you
could no longer navigate around.
You had to force a change in her.
Now was the time, she had to conform.
For now, that was all that was consuming your mind.
More and more every day she watched you knowing the signs,
even as you lied to her, that all was fine.
You swore that you would never leave her, as others had done,

even as she knew that you were being untrue.
You not only lied to her, but you also lied to yourself.
For as you sought to change her,
The only one you changed, was you.
For this is how...... you kill a butterfly.
Even as unknowingly, you held her world in your hands.
Yet you refused to even see her, for all that she was.
All that mattered to you, was what you wanted.
Not what you already held within your hands.
But what you had been told you deserved,
of what you should be looking for instead.
So much more or so much better, than her now.
You would have never been satisfied.
You wanted more and more, no matter how hard she tried.
Yet only too late, did you come to realize.
You had held the world, in the palm of your hand,
only to trade it for something, only in your dreams.
In dreams in which
you would never see or understand, would never materialize.
Only too late, do you realize you willingly gave the moon away
while reaching for the stars.
For all that you had been told to look for,
was not what you wanted in life.
The grass was not greener on the other side.
You missed her.
The ones who convinced you to make a change.
They were no longer around.
They had gone back to their own lives now that
they had destroyed your world, as it was.
You have no one to share your day with,
no one to come home to.
Where were the reasons to change, were
they important to you now?
Where is the excitement you expected to find?
What were you looking to discover?

That you were missing her?
What else did you need in your life?
Only now do you realize
all that you were looking for, you had already attained.
Where do you go, from where you are now? What do you say?
What will you do as reality sinks in?
Sitting with that cup of morning coffee, remembering.
Can you even remember why, you needed that change?
Does it matter so much now?
Where are all the ones that stressed the importance
of that change?
And as you sit here alone, wondering why?
How had it gotten this far? How did this happen?
Losing sight of life so fast?
Did it really matter? What will you do now?
Now that you have figured it all out.
Exactly......how to kill a butterfly.
Where do you go now?

Laurie 2020

I Apologize, But...

I make no apologies, for who I am,
even while saying sorry, every five minutes,
apparently.
I may apologize, for the air I breathe,
the past, or what I might say next.
But I'll never apologize, for the woman I've become.
I have earned that right, the hard way.
I have not always made the best choices,
said the best things, or showed the best side of myself
but I will own up to every single decision,
I have ever made in my life, good or bad.
They're a part of my past.
I can't change that, and even if I could,
I would never wish to.
I'm sure if in my stubbornness, I chose
to make the mistakes before
I would in my own obnoxious self,
think I could fix it and probably do much worse,
if I had the chance to try and change the past.
All of which culminates into the present person, that I am today.
I do my best to lead by example, to make
the most of the time here.
I enjoy life and make it the best, of what it can be.
My blunt honesty has a bitter sting at times.
My advice will be harsh some days.
Also, don't ask me if you don't want my blunt answers.
But my intentions are well meaning and innocent.
I will never hurt someone purposefully.
But in my ignorance, I have hurt people,
sometimes unknowingly, which isn't excusable either.
But that hurt, was never part of my intention.
That's not to say I haven't ever caused pain,

I'm sure I have caused deep pain to some.
I am human after all, flaws, and all,
stitched imperfectly together.
And for any collateral damage left in the fallout,
I truly am sorry if you were ever caught up in that landslide
of emotions from time to time.
I apologize.
At the end of the day, I am who I am,
and I have worked hard
to get here.
I give my all to anything, that I am doing,
and I live my life to the fullest,
with my heart and soul completely
each and every day.
Life is too short to have regrets or to wish
I had taken that chance.
It is meant to be lived,
so, take me as I am with all the mistakes,
broken pieces, cracks, and Imperfections.
Or don't take me at all.
It's all a part of me either way,
whether you choose to accept it or not.
What you see is what you get.
Scars, blemishes, mistakes.
There are no false pretenses here.
So....I will make my apologies in advance,
because I know they will be needed in time.
So, I apologize
But...... not for a life.

Laurie, 2022

If For Just a Day

I can see you've been hurt,
though not a bruise will show.
You've cried endless tears, I know.
That you have been broken in ways,
that can't even be explained.
The bitterness you feel growing deep inside,
that you pushed away with trembling hands,
the pain you've always wiped away, with your tears.
Past the anguish, I see
you found your smile
and you have learned to laughed again.
Somehow your eyes still light up, in the spring rain.
Your ability to smile through the tears
makes you that much more beautiful to me,
you've always found a way to rise from the ashes
of a broken heart.
Like a phoenix away, with a burst of light.
Try as they might, they could never clip those wings
as you have risen above so many things.
Those tears that roll down your ivory cheeks.
They weren't for you, were they?
You wept for them, as you knew they would soon find out,
but much too late,
that they were lost more than you had ever been.
They didn't deserve you
even on their best day,
and you didn't deserve that torment on your worst.
With charisma, grace, and strength,
as you rose and walked away with a smile,
you embodied all the ideals
that no one quite ever understood about you.
They couldn't see past the smiles and the laughter.

The sparkle that had shown, but never quite reached your eyes.
The woman they thought they knew,
but they knew nothing, about you at all.
You played your part, and you played it well,
assembling a wall around your heart,
a convincing facade for the world to see.
You did it to protect your heart and stay strong
for everyone else, you held so dear.
Because that's just who you are.
You were never given a choice, to be anyone else.
There's no need to hide your truth from me.
For I see past the smile, and I see the pain in your eyes.
Through the thinly veiled wall of tears.
Past the storm clouds that protects your soul.
You have fought to become, who you are.
That smile will always be your signature, for the world to see.
A marvelous tribute to your courage, your
dignity, and your inner beauty.
You've never looked back and regretted it, but
sometimes I know loneliness can be overwhelming.
Sometimes you stop laughing, because you're just
trying to survive, and that takes all your strength.
At times, the night may be beautiful,
but in the silence of twilight,
is a deafening silence of worries, thoughts, of past days,
lost love and many painful memories.
I see you, past the smile you wear for the world.
I feel your soul.
I feel the sadness at times, not for the woman
you want the world to see,
but for the magnificent person that you are,
the one that you hide so deep.
I know you thought for so long, that you could never
find someone who could see the real you.
The you that no one else ever sees.

And you didn't. He saw you first.
For that reason, he will never be the same again.
Neither is perfect,
but you can be perfectly imperfect together.
You don't have to be afraid, sad, or lonely anymore.
You won't be alone now or ever again.
He can't promise you the moon or stars, or even
that he will never make a mistake,
but he can promise you
that you will never have to face the storms alone, not anymore.
With that promise that he will never stop loving you
or giving your heart, his absolute best.
I know that you're never too old,
to start believing in magic.
I know I'm not.
It won't be easy, and it won't be fast.
But with love in your hearts and courage in your souls,
You can take this journey.
You and the one you love.
One step at a time.
I can't promise you won't stumble or lose your way,
but if you face it together,
I can promise it will always be worth it.
Worth the long wait
if but, for just a day.

Laurie 2022

That Old Pine

I had just finished crossing the valley and came to stand.
High above the fragrant field.
The air filled with the remnants of the past.
The present, and of times yet to come.
I was on my way towards Current River,
following the sound of the water.
I hear it rushing and flowing over the rocks
with the sound like music to my ears.
I cannot see it, but I know I'm close.
Although it's been many years passed,
I have yearned for that sound, this moment in time.
If only, in my mind
Now, as I walk across the ridge, she comes within my sight.
So many years have passed, so many nights
yearning for her sound and the colors that play,
along the surface of her waters.
She's calmly flowing today, leaves swirling along on the
surface, moving along with the different currents
that make up this beautiful river, but She's not like this always.
As I walked just past the big rock formation that lies just ahead
around the curve in the path,
suddenly another of nature's wonders captures
my attention and I slow my pace.
So many memories of this place
so, I stopped for a moment, just to observe
its curves and angles, the way the years have changed
and molded this tree.
It must have been just a seedling, so many years ago.
A lifetime it seems, as I stand pondering her.
Many years spent through the wind and driving rains,
possibly heavy snow,
this massive white pine laying claim to all that lies within

her shade.
Oh my, how she has grown her mighty branches reaching
out over the banks of the Current River.
I had so keenly sought for a sight of the river,
never giving a thought to what I might see along the way.
I had only meant to walk this way, for one reason,
but now I realize, the very creation of God
stands in this old path, where I had once walked.
No matter what season lay upon this land, is under this
majestic lady's observance, for she is to be the protector of all.
Many who have sought her shelter,
down through the many years.
She has offered a soft, fragrant bed of her pine needles
lying all around her, upon the forest floor.
For any that passes by, for just a moment or more,
She touches the heavens, with the wispy branches
the way only a tall pine tree can do
as to her roots grown deep, showing strength enough
to endure all seasons,
the fragrant smell of pine tar flowing down from her bark.
Her life as well has been a harsh one.
She's known for many years, hopefully many more to come.
She knows deep within, when to stand and fall
to ultimately make way for those yet to come.
Her stature is important in whatever
form she happens to exist in,
as she keeps rising up from the Earth.
One day she will have to return from whence she came.
But in the meantime,
she will stand alongside the Ole Current River.
I was then drawn to stand close and listen to the sounds.
I had never forgotten the peace that had always settled
over my mind.
Then as I looked back at that old white pine, I realized this tree
is an important part of the past too.

As I remember from years ago,
the seedlings scattered out across the forest floor.
It's taking my mind back in time, remembering the paths
we could take on our way down to the riverbank,
following old ones, making new ones all along the way.
I know that I will visit again in another season, possibly in
another time, if no other way maybe, just in my memories.
Just through the flashes in my mind, watching
as her seasons come and go.
As the branches, at certain time's outlined in the fallen
snow, soft and wispy against the setting sun.
When the temperature is cool or then again hot, I
have come to realize no matter the season here,
She will be in my favorite spot to dream of
and be a part of in my mind.
Of all the memories I have kept locked away, even if she falls,
I will always remember her by this river
as part of a fond, childhood memory,
a dream that I still visit from time to time.
For what do we have
if we don't have the memory of the past,
of the special moments we keep close?
What would we have without those?

Laurie 2022

I Have Always Heard It Said

You should not judge people's character
based solely, upon the gossip of others.
They seem ready to spread careless words so easily.
Any gossip about an innocent person.
Never wanting to find out exactly why,
those people are spreading that gossip.
Why someone may want to hurt them, in that way?
For gossip from a damaged heart
or an emotional moment in time,
Will be regretted, sometimes as soon as it's spoken,
Or once the issue is resolved, or the hurt of the moment is over.
But careless words spoken out of turn,
will live on in infamy, so long after the heartache is over.
Never realizing they are leaving the person the gossip is about
to deal with the damage of the fallout
for many years afterwards,
therefore.... hurting an innocent party in many aspects.
Through the ignorance of someone,
that speaks out of hurt or disappointment.
Maybe that person didn't agree with their point of view
and it was easier to talk about them,
than shoulder the blame themselves,
for a discussion gone wrong.
Some people can never simply say "That
was my fault Or I'm sorry".
It's so much easier to look innocent
and paint the other party, as the guilty one.
That is so their image stays untarnished to everyone else,
which seems to be so particularly important,
to a lesser person, it seems.
Yet in most cases, the person
the gossip is about

will never speak out, nor will ever say anything,
about the other person.
Integrity is usually humble or quiet,
they don't need to be heard.
Not like the one who seems to have the need,
for everyone to know
their side so badly.
They want all the blame to lie with the quiet one.
They feel the need for everyone to be aware
that they were never at fault and how they were done so wrong.
That is something they need to broadcast quickly,
just to keep their image intact.
Yet never realizing at the time, how petty they are
and how selfish that moment in time makes them look.
They are quick to point out all they have done or
how much money they may have spent.
Yet never seeming to acknowledge, the amount of time
the other has spent or the help,
that money could never have been equal too.
Or the energy the other party may have spent
making their lives easier, while they were there.
It's better to paint them as a taker, as a selfish person
to make known, there was no return in kind.
Rather than someone that gave all they had and was there,
for everything that was needed.
This way makes them look so much better,
they seem to think.
Yet in reality, they came across as petty, ungrateful beings
that was never in that relationship for any of the right reasons.
Maybe the gossiped about party, made them feel important
and they felt admired, when some asked
if they were with them.
Or maybe they had expectations other
than what there was, in their relationship.
For so many factors, hurt pride

will never allow them to acknowledge,
they might have been wrong.
But people who walk beside you during the hard times,
deserve to have a place next to you, during the better times.
Also, again, I have always heard it said …
when people talk behind your back
it must be because you are so much more,
than they could have ever dreamed of being.
And thought provokes jealousy,
and they don't even seem to be able to understand why.
When you refuse to engage or respond in kind,
that makes them so much worse,
but never stoop to their level,
that only makes you seem petty and insecure.
I have come to realize one of the most motivational moments
in your life,
It's when you achieve something that everyone told you
that you will never do.
You have carried out the impossible in their eyes.
But to be honest, it is more in time that we realize our decisions
and actions affect a lot of people around us.
Sometimes those effects aren't known until years later.
I know now that you can lose everything and everyone.
As long as you never lose hope, your integrity and faith.
Simply never allow anyone to tell you to dim your light
let them buy sunglasses if they can't take the shine.
You just keep shining.
You must never diminish yourself
to make someone else feel better.
That's their problem, not yours.
Remember that somewhere in the middle of our ordinary lives,
you may be completely surprised or blindsided, with a fairytale.
Only share yourself with the people,
who you know deserves to have some of your amazingness.
Learn to appreciate what you can offer the world.

You are an amazingly unique individual with talents
that are just your own, makes you different.
When you feel you're lost, keep looking up.
Truly, because that is when you will find yourself.
When you share love, adventures, and life with others,
always remember that you deserve that same love, for yourself.
We get so involved in taking care of
and doing for everyone else,
we forget that we count too.
Know that we can't all do great things, all the time.
Yet we can all do little things, with great love all the time.
Your thoughts are like a mirror.
You can always adjust it, make it clearer,
but always be careful of selfish people.
When you give your hand, they will grab your arm
and end up stepping on your face
without even an apology.
It's just expected.
When you thank God every day, for what you already have,
you will be blessed with more of what you need.
There's a huge difference between need and want.
I know, that when people walk away from you,
it will break your heart,
yet in the end it will save your soul.
It may not feel like you have accomplished much
or any accomplishments, are showing right now.
But keep in mind, when you get to the top and look back,
you will see how far you have come.
You may feel alone at times, but it is much worse to feel alone,
in a room full of people.
Never substitute people for contentment.
You will never need someone to complete you.
You must learn to enjoy being alone with yourself.
Before you can ever know contentment with anyone else.

Laurie 2022

A Heart Breaking

I have known sheer hopelessness,
helpless to get away from the weight of it all.
I have known and seen raw emotions looking back at me
from my own mirror, thru dark and empty eyes.
Each morning as I see the same eyes looking back at me
as if they have something to say,
yet unable to hold the pain back long enough,
to find spoken words.
I have known the pain of loss so deep
that I stand and fight
just to control the simple feat of each and every gasping breath
as I stand and try to steady
the ragged beat of a broken heart.
Some days needing a map to navigate in this world,
so unaware of what I'm trying to process.
All just so I can prepare and cover my emotions
enough, to make it through the day.
Just to be able to carry on this charade,
of being in control of my own life
as I keep trying to find a rhythm.
Just to make it through the day in public,
so, I can make it home
to fall apart in private,
just make it back to my sanctuary
where I can relax and just be me.
Have you ever known complete and utter exhaustion?
Physically, emotionally, even spiritually exhausted
so much that it can't be slept off or brushed away,
no matter how many tears that have fallen
or how many times you put yourself back together,
yet no one ever suspects a thing
as I hid it all, behind that smile.

I greet them, as if all is well and nothing has ever happened.
I have spent so many days and nights
yearning for a single reprieve.
Just one.
That's all I ask for, yet I still have something to atone for,
it seems
as I stand in awe,
I marvel at how much a soul can yearn, to be whole again,
to be put back together again.
Or just to have someone to listen to
without a fear
of broken trust or gossip coming back to your ears later.
Coming back for you to hear, over and over again.
Just that someone to understand,
just to sit and relax with the ability to decipher
what can't be spoken into mere words.
Yet you know that no matter how many times
you have trusted and tried,
it always comes back to haunt you.
So, you never speak those unspoken words and fears.
Never share the emotions or thoughts
tumbling and churning
in your mind.
You see me standing, as if I'm too proud to sit,
yet you never realize the reason why,
you, see?
If I allow myself to get comfortable or relax my guard,
I will possibly fall apart.
I know this from the deepest part of me
down to the marrow of my bones that support me.
Do you ever wonder? Do you ever stop and ask?
If so, when a heart breaks,
do you see the shards lying all around?
Does it make a sound you can hear?
Or is it only in my mind?

This deafening explosion of emotions I hear inside of myself,
as it drowns and cancels out any and all,
that is happening around me.
Yet looking at me now, you would never know.
I'm sure it seems that I have it all figured out
and seem to be in control of all, that is around me.
Such is the grand illusion of life that we must create,
for appearance's sake.
Ah, but for you to be a fly on the wall
in the early morning hours
as sleep evades my tired mind,
then you would be asking yourself, these same questions.
Like if a heart is breaking and no one else is around,
will it still make a sound?

Laurie 2022

Her Own Way

She knows she has my own way of doing things.
Her own way of living.
A completely different life.
She has never been the usual and ordinary or even normal.
So far from it, in some ways.
That's what makes her who she is.
Learning to be happy
and finding more fulfillment
in whom she has grown to be,
has become the normal for her.
Truthfully, most people that she has met,
didn't understand her at all.
And because of that,
she stays mostly to herself,
purely out of self-preservation.
Avoidance of the "normal,"
finding her abnormal in their minds.
Most around her,
would have rather embrace the unusual confines
of their comfort zones,
rather than step out into the unknown.
That is the danger, she represented.
They would smile and say, "she's just a bit different" Isn't she?
"But she has a beautiful way about her, who she
is and uncompromising in her character.
She stands for what she believes in and follows her heart
almost to a fault.
She is not afraid to put herself out there
and risk her heart to chase her dreams and desires.
She's never going to be the one living for
tomorrow and playing it safe, will she?
She's a wild creature, unafraid to do the unthinkable.

She fights to be herself and be free.
Maybe she'll take a trip, without a destination on any given day.
Perhaps dancing outside in the rain, when begins to storm,
rain drops, falling freely upon her face,
as she turns with her face into the wind and up towards the sky.
Maybe she will go somewhere, she's never been
just to see where she needs to be.
Experiencing the people, the places, the adventures
she finds, all along the way."
"To be free in a way that most will never understand
or ever have the courage to be, the very definition of her.
And she is more than okay, with that kind of life.
It makes her soul happy, living her best life and being
the authentic loving and fun-loving person, she is.
That's a lot of great people
doing amazing things out there in this life, to be sure.
But once you meet her, you will never forget her.
For she is more than just a pretty face, more than
just a person or an interesting character.
She's a brave and passionate soul
that can change your life.
Only if you're ready to let go
of who you are and embrace who you might
become, with her at your side.
That's who she will always be.
Fiery, unique, and free, just the way she'll always want to be.
She'll never settle for less."
Then they might smile and shake their head, as they walk away.
They even might be heard to say, "She just scares
a man to death, but maybe someday, she will
find someone that can keep up with her."
But in her own mind, she knows that will never be.
For who would accept for who she is?
Who she had fought so hard to be?
No one, they all expect her to change,

and for that she can never concede.
For to change herself now, would be to lose who she is
and all that she has fought so hard, to be.
To make her normal again,
she would have to admit defeat,
losing all ground, she has covered,
becoming the same boring image of all she sees.
And that is someone, she can never be again.
For this very reason she knows,
she may always walk alone.

Laurie 2022

Still, I Would Have Chosen You

I still would have chosen you.
Even before you were born, had I gone to heaven,
if even but in my dreams and saw all
other beautiful little ones there.
I still would have chosen you
If God had told me this child would one day require extra care.
I would have had long days, sleepless nights,
fulfilling those needs.
I still would have chosen you
If he had told me this child, may make your heart bleed,
make you question yourself, even me.
I still would have chosen you
If he had told me, this child would make you question
the depths of your faith or even possibly my grace.
I still would have chosen you
If he had told me, this child would make
tears flow from my eyes
that some days could have filled a river.
I still would have chosen you
If he had told me, this child may one day
make you feel overwhelming suffering, anguish,
and make you question everything; to live.
I still would have chosen you
If he had told me, all that you know to be normal
would drastically change.
Nothing will ever be the same if this child is the one you choose.
I still would have chosen you
Of course,
even though, I would always have chosen you.
I know it was God,
who chose me for you.

For me to be a mother, to these special little boys.
Even still, I would have chosen you.

Laurie 2022

To Nick and Jared, with all my Love.
Love Mom

Just Me

I used to lie awake all night
with so many thoughts
and worries going through my mind.
Each one, with a new scenario,
bringing to me a new nightmare,
time after time.
I was spending my time at night,
the time meant for rest,
tossing and turning over what new horrors,
tomorrow might bring.
Over how the day before had gone.
What might I have changed or done
in a different way for a better outcome?
I would worry about what could have happened,
what might happen, and everything in between.
My brain would overthink and overanalyze everything
to the point of sheer exhaustion.
Unable to sleep or rest
because I couldn't shut my mind off
or filter out the thoughts and worries.
All of the what ifs?
I would spend so much energy, on the possibilities of tomorrow,
until I had nothing left for today.
Until living that way finally broke me.
Broken into countless pieces from worrying
and letting my thoughts and fears, get the best of me.
I finally realized that I couldn't keep going on this way.
And though it wasn't easy, and it still isn't,
I found a way past all the anxiety of tomorrow's unknowns.
Truly, I thought back to all the times,
when the worst times, in my life happened.
I was always fine, on the other side of that.

I always made it through, so to speak.
I have always managed to find a way to overcome,
adapt and keep going.
That's the moment, that I finally understood.
The truth of it was,
that the stress I was causing myself
wasn't going to change anything.
But no matter what, I'd always be okay.
Maybe it wouldn't be pretty,
maybe it wouldn't always turn out the way I expected it to be.
But I could handle anything.
I had proven that to myself time and time again.
I am not going to say,
that I do not overthink life anymore,
because that will never truly go away.
But I've learned not to let the worry,
consume my mind anymore.
I had been letting my thoughts and worries control me.
Instead of me having to be in charge,
of what I was thinking and feeling, every little detail.
I slowly, have become okay,
with letting the future be unknown.
I found some peace hidden
within the storms of life.
My days aren't always easy, and I will always
have plenty of challenges.
But now, I can keep it in its own perspective
and not let the bad thoughts
ruin my good days.
It can rain, even downpour,
but I finally learned, how to start dancing in the rain,
letting the flashes of lightning show me the path,
as the Thunder lets me know, I am still okay.
So, as I walk along and cruise through my day

strong, proud, Independent, and free.
For now, I realize,
That is just me.

Laurie 2022

Thoughts

I just want to say, please be careful with your words.
For once they are spoken and once these words are said
they can only be forgiven, but never forgotten.
How you make others feel about themselves with your words,
will say a lot about you, to them.
Do not say something permanently hurtful,
just because you are temporarily upset.
It only takes a few moments to hurt someone with our words,
but it can take a lifetime to repair the damage done,
in that careless moment of irritation.
Be sure to taste your words, before you spit them out.
Think how you would feel if they were spoken to you.
Do not mix bad words, with a bad mood.
You will have many opportunities to change your mood,
but not an opportunity to retrieve the words
you may have spoken.
Speak only when you feel your words
are better
than your silence.
You never know how long your words
will stay in someone else's mind
long after you have forgotten them.
Just because you're free to say whatever you want
doesn't mean that you always should.
So, before you give someone your opinion,
or a piece of your mind, stop for a moment and breathe,
take a second to think.
Then feel your words against your own skin,
the weight of them on your tongue,
in your own heart.
For when your foot slips,

you can always recover your balance.
But when your tongue slips,
you can never recover your words.

Laurie, 2022

What My Heart Craves

I was not born to be easily managed or tamed.
I have always been known as someone
caught in between faraway dreams and reality.
I thrive in controlled chaos, as a moth to a flame.
As a wildfire,
when it pulls the air in and releases its flames,
with a fury rivaled by nothing created by man......
As a hurricane with a calm center, in the eye of the storm.
Yet it will cost your heart and soul to escape.
Always loving the rain, but it never seemed
to be a light summer rain.
It was always with a wild wind,
as the waves climbed higher and higher.
That was the storm, I would be drawn to,
the heavy rains pouring down the face of the rock,
ice crystals forming upon crests of the
waves, driven in by the winds.
My heart could find its answers,
in the pounding of the waves against the cliffs.
That is where I could be found, even now.
For all that wild chaos of nature, is what my heart craves.
For a space in time, in which the fury cannot be tamed.
For my chaos to be answered,
in a storm of this magnitude
of which can cover the sound
of my own storms inside.
Drowning out the sound of my own hearts pounding
in time with the crashing of the waves.
This is what my heart cries for, a place and time
in which it cannot be tamed or contained, just to exist.
For when you look for me, that is where you will find me.
For that is what my heart craves.

Laurie, 2022

If You Think

If you think you have already been beaten,
you are and will continue to be.
If you think you could never dare,
you never will.
Terrified of the change or of taking the chance?
Then you never will.
If you want to win, but you know you can't,
it's almost a certainty, you won't.
If you think you will lose, you've already lost.
For in this world, we live in, we find success in life
begins with a person's outlook,
on their life.
With the determination, with which they wish to live.
It all begins and ends with the state of mind.
If you think you are outclassed and will never be enough,
you are, and you never will be.
You must think, you can rise, and you will stand.
You must be in control of yourself and of your emotions,
before you can change the outcome of your life.
You can never win the prize if you never take the time to try.
Life's battles will not always go to the stronger or faster person.
But sooner or later when you win,
it is because you were the one, who knew you would.
No matter how long the road or steep that mountain,
always believe that you will make it to the top.
No matter how many times you must get up,
always believe you can.
The only way you can lose
is if you fail to try.

Laurie 2022

Tapestry of Life

If you think you will know who she is
when you meet her,
think again.
She might look just like an ordinary girl on the outside,
but she is a guarded one.
Yes?
That's because on the inside,
She is so different, than anyone else.
So, who she really is will shock you.
You will see that smile.
She will be courteous
and always have a friendly,
collected look as she engages you, in conversation.
She seems so sweet and gentle.
But make no mistake.
If you decide to push her
just a little too far out of her comfort
zone or try stepping on her,
you will see a side of her that will change
your mind, in an instant.
A side, that you will never forget,
For all you will be left with, will just be regret.
She's not who she is now, because she wanted to be.
She never wanted to be this guarded,
sometimes distant creature,
but she is because life chose this path for her.
She was never asked or consulted about
when her life would become this way.
She did not ever want to be so consumed, with the
thoughts of survival, learning to fight and scrape,
just to survive her days.
But that's the hand she's been dealt, her cards in life.

As some would say.
Broken and battered, she wanted to give up many times.
just to lay down her heart and walk away.
But she is not one to give up, not on any given day.
When you suffer long enough, losing repeatedly.
Eventually your soul grows weary.
It begins to beg you to just give in.
But that's where she was for way too long.
Tired, lost, anxious, and afraid to step out,
trying to keep her head just above water,
just to take the next ragged breath.
She didn't yet, know how to pick herself back up, when she fell.
She still couldn't find any answers, she
was just looking for a light,
to dissipate the darkness, which surrounded her in life.
But it wasn't even those moments of struggle, that defined her.
It was just the opposite, you see.
Finally, she dug herself out of that place
and clawed her way back up, out of that void.
That, my friends, is what has really defined her,
Combined with her insistent drive to keep going,
growing, and eventually even thriving.
And finally, learning to live as she is now.
She has faced the fires of her choices in life,
stumbling through the tragedies, and decided she was
so much more than any of that.
She has not allowed that to define her, as she has molded and
shaped her life to something she could look at with pride.
Looking back now and knowing how far she has come.
More than capable, she is more than the hardships,
which brought her down burning fiercer than the fire
that had threatened to tear her apart.
Her courage and determination, were forged in the flames
of those defining moments.
She's not brave, because she wanted to be.

She's brave because she had to be.
Sometimes you don't choose what
you become; it chooses you.
She's a survivor, never a victim.
She's a warrior with an iron will and a passionate spirit,
an unending desire to succeed and thrive.
So, when you cross paths with this amazing woman,
don't assume you know her or ever think
you know, what she's been through.
Simply appreciate who she is and where she's been,
even where she is going.
You may never understand her, but you don't have to.
She is who she is, unapologetically and without regret.
It is what it is.
That is her code, she lives by now.
She celebrates her flaws, while her scars tell her story.
And it's an amazing tale of beautiful and brutal
survival, one of immeasurable courage.
She is so much more than the fires, that once consumed her,
her wings are meant for more, than simple flight.
Wild creatures like her cannot be contained, defined, or tamed.
We can only hope to enjoy them, just the way they are.
For she was never truly broken, never completely
beaten down, never totally defeated.
Just a breathtaking, chaotic muse, a beautiful mosaic
depicting the battles she won along her journey.
She will always be what others, will never understand.
Some will hate her, while many will fall in love
with whom they think, she is.
Most will never really know her, only the side she shows.
Each will see a different person, in her
strong will, beautiful soul,
a total contradiction of emotions,
colors and moods.
As a butterfly, she will never stay in one place,

but she will leave her mark, wherever she lands.
Touching the lives around her and
leaving her memory behind.
In this tapestry
that she calls life.

Laurie, 2022

Only in The Quiet

It will never be just her words, which will tell her story.
Instead, it will be her silence.
Her silence, that will speak volumes, booming in the quiet.
You can read her heart, mind, body, and soul, thru her eyes.
But only in the quiet, that is when you will hear her.
Sometimes the rest, cannot heal a weary heart.
Though her mind is alive and spirited.
Her soul is tired.
Her heart is broken in her depth.
She is weary.
Her spirit is bone tired in a way, that sleep cannot remedy,
nor could she explain it to you, even if she tried.
Her eyes show her truths, where her words cannot.
Sometimes she hides all her anguish and love behind a smile.
Yet it will never quite reach her eyes if
you take the time to notice.
For she hides herself behind the walls,
she has built around her world to protect herself.
It hides her away from this world, she has overcome.
From all the past heartache and struggle.
Some days she carries herself, as with a soul forged of fire.
With a raw form of courage born of necessity,
so don't expect her to tear those walls down easily.
She fought valiantly for who she is now
and for what she has.
So, she will break apart her ship, upon the shores of solitude
before she ever allows someone else, that close to her heart.
So now, when you hear what she says,
and you find yourself trying to understand her words.
Do more to understand her actions or how she withdraws
Into her own little world.

Just know that her spoken and even her
unspoken truth, is her greatest pride.
And the most fiercely prized part of herself,
is her brutal honesty and her solitude.
She'll put on a brave smile and a gentle facade
because that is how she survives, those hardest days.
On pure bravado and strength of her will to forge ahead.
But just realize, she did not choose to be this way.
Life pushed her across the broken road,
destroying her along the way.
Even while she learned to survive,
and somehow, she found a way to thrive
and grow in the process.
The truth is, she does not want or need anyone to
understand who she is, behind those closed doors.
Her heart is just too fragile, to risk being broken again.
Deep down, she wants to love, but she is afraid the next person,
will be just like the last one,
who broke her before.
So, she is content to live her life and
celebrate her small victories.
Helping her loved ones along the way,
in the simple ways of her life.
She does not need fanfare or attention to be happy.
She just needs contentment, peace, serenity, and honesty.
So, before you knock on the door to her soul,
know that she is a beautiful mess.
Like the rainbows edge.
Shining in the middle of a hurricane.
Just a beautifully broken disaster.
Know that she will never be easy to love.
Nor will she ever settle for less.
Although one thing is for certain.
Her soulful depths and gentle love will be unforgettable,
and no matter what,

she will stand loyal to her word, should you ever win her heart.
She will always be worth any price; you may have to pay.
The time you spend with her, will never be a waste.
For the time it will take to uncover the
true beauty of a woman like this,
is time that will be well spent.
For the one that holds her hand, who
brings that smile to her eyes.
Is the one that will hold the keys to her heart.

Laurie, 2022

Just Be

She sat at the back of the room, quietly, taking it all in.
She could hear the whispers.
They said she was too quiet and shy,
she would never make it
in real life.
So, she bravely tried to lead from the front,
cautiously, taking the attention of the crowd in her hands.
She was taking the lead, while making a stand.
Then they hated her for her pride and resented her,
for stepping out.
They asked her for her advice and then loudly,
questioned her guidance, as she walked away.
Even said, "that she thinks she knows better than any of us."
Then she was branded rude and loud
when she spoke up in defense of someone else,
when they could not speak for themselves.
With their words, they hammered her to the ground,
but were shocked into silence by her quiet authority,
as she simply said
"Enough is enough" continuing to stand her ground.
When she shared no ambitions or dreams with them,
they said it was sad.
She was going nowhere with her life.
Oh, but they could not see, what she saw in her dreams.
Yet when she told them of her dreams.
They branded her as weird and eccentric,
living in an unknown reality.
Or she was just simply crazy, would
never fit in with normal people.
They told her they would listen.
Yet they walked away, covering their ears when she spoke.
Never understanding her level of wisdom,

for she spoke in terms they could never comprehend,
in their narrow minds.
Some would give her an insincere hug,
while laughing at her fears, shaking
their heads at her innocence.
Simply saying, that she might not be strong
enough, to make it in the real world.
And she listened to all of it, thinking she should
give up on her dreams even then.
Truly never knowing, she was so much more,
than they thought she could be.
She had always tried to be the girl,
they all told her she should be,
as best as she could anyway.
Until that one day she was asked,
"What the best for herself was?"
then to her surprise, there was no ready answer.
She had to pause for a moment and think
of all the years spent trying to please everyone else.
Trying to be someone else, someone
she was not meant to be.
Only to find out, she would never fit in.
And in that moment, she realized,
she never knew who she was
or who she wanted to be.
So, she walked to the river and stood
silently, amongst the trees.
She could actually hear the wind whisper and dance,
above her within the leaves.
As she stood watching them fall softly
to land upon the surface of the sparkling
water, of the nearby stream.
Watched them gently follow the swirls,
as they floated downstream.
She spoke softly to that wispy Weeping Willow,

as if it should be able to read her mind.
Leaning her back against the Elm, using it as her strength, as
she felt the weight of her world settle down, upon her shoulders.
With a deep breath, smelling the pungent
fragrance of the White Pine.
As the sun began to set, she softly told them
all of her heartaches and fears, she would
disappoint all the people that she loved.
Time after time, she had been told to fit in
and stop searching for more, to lay down her
dreams and be happy with her reality.
She told them of how she felt that she was never enough,
yet sometimes too much, all at the same time.
She was either too little or too small to make the difference.
Where she went too far and beyond what was needed.
When her laugh was too loud or too quiet.
Her demeanor too fierce, then sometimes too weak.
There seemed to never be an equal balance to anything.
Her counsel wise, or too foolish.
Her voice too bold or too meek.
No one would listen to her speak.
Then she began to walk.
Till she found a small clearing surrounded by wild ferns.
There she stopped, and she heard, what the breeze
whispered back to her.
She listened to the birds as they bantered above her.
Fluttering about high in the trees.
It is there, that she rested and let all worries fall away,
as she had said all.
All that she needed to say.
She sat for hours, not wanting to ever leave that place
The peace settling softly over her,
surrounding her in quiet.
For the forest had nothing to say.
It was just letting her breathe.

For to the forest,
she was all it needed her too be.
And that was enough for her,
To just be.

Laurie 2022

Kassius V. Klipfel

10/19/2021

You have rested his life, within our hands.
Allowing us to protect him and raise him strong.
Allowing us the chance to celebrate his life.
To teach him songs,
teach him how to live, right from wrong.
To never take a single moment for granted.
For we all know that time moves so fast,
and someday soon, he will not be so small.
He will grow, to be a strong young man.
But you know, we will do our best to try and teach him,
to always hold on to your hands.
Still, I am sure he will slip and when he does,
we will need you to soften his fall.
There will be long dark nights when
he will need your strength.
His life will have burdens, which will be
hard for him to bear alone.
He will get a taste of life.
He will find love and play into the hands of fate.
He will have days when he thinks he is not enough.
That he can no longer walk strong,
he will feel he has not strength left, to carry on.
But in those moments, give use the wisdom to leave him
in your hands.
As you will be there to remind him, of his own strengths,
of his future and your promises, to see
him through his hard days.
This special little boy, you have given us the privilege to raise.
Please Lord, give us the strength
to stay faithful and strong

for this little boy, Kassius V. Klipfel
An incredibly special one
October 19th, 2021

Laurie

Learning To Live Again

Healing and insanity really does not ever have an end.
I realize, as I am letting things go all over again.
Just to move forward, to find them again and again.
Broken pieces are scattered all around me,
but they are aligning, moving together
with the pieces that fit or can be made to fit now.
Life remains fluid, constantly changing,
moving through the seasons, as I heal and grow.
With those many painful, yet needful changes.
Each day puts me to a different kind of challenge,
a different environment, a whole new way.
Different ways to deal with those jagged pieces,
that I carry around with me
each and every day.
I never really know, just where my mind will go,
where my day will take me, or who I will meet.
Some I may have known before.
But I meet again, in this new era of my life.
I never know what my eyes will see or what rhythm
my heart will decide to beat to, on any given day.
I never know which shadow or memory, will start ripping at me
when I hear a certain sound.
Catch a whisper of a memory of a voice
or catch a smell in the air.
I never know anything or what will transpire,
as I am fighting off imaginary enemies, in my own mind.
Madness cannot be chosen,
I have found, as it chooses you.
Memories, broken dreams, and all kinds of imaginary things,
targets the broken ones.
The ones the bell never rings for
or has already rung through, in times past.

You cannot evolve into insanity, from sanity.
Insanity evolves into you.
Crashing within your mind, as harsh waves to the shore.
Each one harder and harder, as you silently scream,
for the truth to be found.
Or you just beg for nothing more.
A twisted menagerie of thoughts destroying
everything around you.
As your dreams come crashing, bringing those carefully
constructed walls down, around all you have built.
Tsunamis of shattered memories, forgotten
emotions or dreams never realized.
Drowning in the chaos, that it always leaves behind.
You go on never realizing a release is
there, just around the corner.
Yet we never seem to go there.
Or get that far.
Instead, you find yourself cutting your
feet, on all the broken glass,
lying scattered all around.
We walk along, never even seeing the shoes lying there.
Beside us on the ground.
Or of that mirror you shattered deep within your own mind,
never seeing through it, to the other side.
Some call it a looking glass.
Some call it a prison.
Some call it a liar, never showing you the truth,
in your own eyes.
I have shattered so many of these mirrors,
then threw them into the fire.
Broken pieces of glass that held all my shattered dreams.
Haunting memories, all kinds of things.
But finally seeing that it was only in my mind.
So, as you look down at your feet, trying to find a path.
Wondering which way to turn, to avoid the most broken glass.

Those reflections will continue.
But only until you realize, it is only in your mind.
A shadow of a once glowing image, a masterpiece of its own.
Right now, it lies in ruins
as you run into the night, looking for a pure form of release.
Some form of a peace of mind,
some kind of answer to all this madness.
You do not want to turn back; yet you really do not want to see.
Instead, running away at full speed.
You will keep running, until you realize
that mirror can't hurt you anymore.
Once you are finally able to see that, you can stop running.
For as on the forest floor, there are no reflections,
only sunlight filtering through the canopy of trees.
You only see the reflections on the
surfaces of the rivers, the lakes,
or on the seas.
On the open waters.
Oh, but only a slight glimmer instead,
as you see the beauty offered
for your eyes to see.
So, beneath the trees you stroll, for there
you have some protection,
as you hide under the falling leaves.
Here you can breathe.
Here you can find some relief.
Here you can be free.
From that mirror that constantly reminds you,
of what only you can see.
For you, see?
You will never really know where your mind will go.
Each day puts on a different kind of slideshow.
It just depends on the memories, which may come along.
But remember, as those broken pieces are aligning and moving
with the pieces that are beginning to fit.

As I am learning,
to start letting things go
as I am finding them again.
It is the right thing to do.
You will also realize,
Insanity really does not have an end.
But it does allow healing and a place, we can begin to grow
and even possibly, a way to learn
to live again.

Laurie 2022

Lessons for life

Some of the hardest lessons, I have learned.
The hard way
You must realize you will never get the apology you would like,
but that is okay.
That person whom you may adore,
may never feel the same about you.
The people you may have sacrificed your happiness for
you realize
they would have never done the same for you.
Being a good person to someone, does not necessarily mean,
they will be good to you in return.
There is no guarantee of that in this life.
Not in today's world.
People will not give you the same respect
as you may give them.
They want you to earn their respect,
while disrespecting you in the process.
Telling someone no and setting boundaries,
possibly doing what is best for you.
That will never set well with the ones, the boundaries are for.
Doing these things will quickly show
you their true nature in itself.
Quit sacrificing your own peace in return,
for what little they give you.
They will never return your love, but
instead, they will harbor ill feelings
of deep-seated resentment
and sometimes hate in their heart for you.
Some will only love you for what you can and will do for them.
Once you stop being of use, their love is gone.
Even though you care so deeply for them.
That will be your downfall and major fault, in doing this.

Just knowing the process, you still will be the one to get hurt,
but that is okay.
Sometimes the people who hug you, as so easily they smile.
Will be the ones holding the knife, as you turn your back.
Make sure that all who you take into your boat,
will be rowing equally and not drilling holes, as you row.
Loyalty is just another word to those people.
Those are the ones for you to feel compassion for,
but to never trust.
For they will never know the true meaning
of that word.
Family is not always about blood.
It is all about who comes into your life and stays,
who is helping and building that trust along the way.
The most valuable thing we have is time.
Use it wisely, for once it is gone, it can never be regained.
There is no returning to that moment in your life.
No one is yours to keep.
Family, children, husband, wife, friends, et cetera.
They will most times stand loyal only to themselves,
and oftentimes that is a different path
than the one you will take.
Saying goodbyes in life will happen
over and over and over again,
but that is okay.
Love them while you have them, so you can
cherish the memories when they leave.
Few people will put you first, unless it is convenient
for them to do so.
Never depend on being their first thought.
It will be a heartbreaking experience.
No one owes you anything.
It is your life, to make it what it is.
Make it the best, that you can make it.
Sometimes you will have to let people walk away,

no matter how many good days, times, or memories
you may have had with them.
You will still stand and watch that door close, behind them.
Lock the door and count your blessings
for the times that you had.
Then you put away that key, never opening that door again.
Very few people will respect your feelings,
they are more concerned, about how you make them feel.
You may never be in that equation.
Humans in general are completely self-centered
and never give much thought to anyone else's wants or needs.
If someone gets hurt,
it will always be them and you will always be at fault
no matter what.
But that is okay.
It is life and it is a good lesson.
Most people will never be grateful for anything.
They will only see what they cannot or what they do not have.
The rest will not matter. It is all about them.
Some will hate you, for being who you are.
You will be a threat, to their standing.
Or maybe we just irritate their demons.
Others will love you, for just being you,
for being the one to step up,
and be the someone, they can always count on.
Sometimes in life you will be unfairly blamed
because it is easier for them to blame someone else,
than have to admit the truth.
Or admit to their own faults.
In other words,
always remember, monsters do not always look the part.
Sometimes they come along looking like the greatest blessing.
Family even, or an old childhood friend.
You may learn that not everyone will care as much as you do.
You may be the weird one.

Some will not be as thoughtful, selfless or as patient
in the times, as you may have been for them.
Not that being this way is better,
it will cause you heartache and pain.
And you will sometimes lose yourself as a person,
ignoring your own feelings, wants, and even needs.
But that is okay.
This world needs more people like that.
You will have to learn to balance.
And you will have to learn to manage
the expectations of others,
while keeping yourself whole.
It is a lifetime of education and lessons in life,
that I speak of, it will be challenging.
Yes, because of your nature
to try and accommodate everyone's needs, around your own
and trying to keep from feeling so much, at the same time.
I have learned, I had to draw lines.
I had to learn these lessons in life, just to survive.
For the way I was, I could be of no more help to myself
or those who surrounded me.
Love and appreciate the ones you are with.
When they speak, take time to listen.
Stop what you are doing and really pay attention to them.
You never know if this will be the last time you see them
or if they will be here tomorrow.
Life is short and very fragile.
Once it is gone, what is left?
We have but this small space in time,
to make a difference in someone's life,
and sometimes we never even realize
that we even did that.
Maybe you were the only one to try.
You cannot save everyone, or even anyone for that matter.
It is up to each and every person to save themselves,

but you can help pave the way for them.
To help in a hard time of need.
You can be the one to hold their hand and just be there
letting them know it is okay.
You will have to be your own hero.
No one is coming on a White Horse to save you.
You will also have to decide to save yourself.
Even though you have spent most of your time,
saving everyone around you,
do not expect the same from them.
Unfortunately, when you need someone,
no one will answer the silent plea for help.
In most cases, no one will be there if you called for help.
Most likely, no one will answer.
People will disappear from your life
when you are no longer of use.
To them, that is just a harsh reality.
We are of use now; therefore, we are loved for now.
But that is okay,
because that's life.
The kinder you are to someone,
the easier it is for them to treat you with disrespect.
Familiarity breeds disrespect or contempt.
Be kind but set firm boundaries.
Trust me, that is said with love and from
too many harsh experiences.
Again, only one that will have a problem with those boundaries.
Will be the people that you have those boundaries for.
Always remember,
most times your family, will be the first to betray you,
quicker than any stranger will.
Being unconditionally loyal to your family,
does not mean they will afford you the same loyalty,
when put into a difficult situation.
You will not be the first choice to save or help,

they will save themselves.
And most times it leaves you to flounder.
It is your job to save them, not vice versa.
Stop expecting yourself, from others.
It does not work that way, and it never will.
Even when you stand up in defense of others
of what you believe is right and true,
it will not keep them from hating you for doing so.
Even if it was done from love, life will change in an instant.
Learn to roll with those waves and you will survive.
Though you may be broken each time, taking longer to heal,
we always survive.
There will always be too few of our kind,
the ones who try to be the better person.
When we do that, we rarely lead an easy life.
We are here to help bring humanity back,
into a harsh world.
Even if in the end it costs us a huge part of ourselves.
It will still be
okay.

Laurie 2022

When My Eyes Are Closed

Like rings of smoke sifting through an empty room,
I feel your love, as it closes in around me.
As I still my heart, its slowly surrounding me,
I feel the world outside, as it seems to just disappear
till you are the only thing that I see.
I have waited so long for this moment, even if but in a memory
Should I say it, or do I dare speak aloud?
So many nights, as if unaware, I reach out to find you.
But there is never really anyone there.
And I have this same dream every night.
Of You here
and somehow you make everything all right.
Each and every time I close my eyes,
And every single day
to the Lord, I pray
that I may just fall back to sleep.
Because who knows, some night,
I may get it right.
If only in my dreams
and this time, your heart.
I could find a way to keep.
Oh, if life were but a dream.
Or is it really?
So, it seems sometimes,
Maybe?
I just do not know.
All I know for sure
is that you will be there, in my dreams.
Every night
When my eyes are closed.

Laurie 2022

My Daddy's Hands

My Daddy's hands are calloused and rough.
They have seen their share of wear and tear.
They have weathered winters, blistered in summers,
and they have bled through every season,
all without a care for his own health or well-being.
Trees have fallen, lumber has been cut, houses built.
His unique designs and newest inventions.
Post driven into the ground, pony carts fixed, concretes mixed.
Seldom did I ever hear a complaint through grease, grime,
muck, and mud.
My Daddy's hands have done it all.
There are no limits to his workdays.
Nothing seems too large or too small.
His days are long, but at the end,
when all of the work is done, he washes
off the busy day with a prayer
in the light of the setting sun.
Now the moment is drawing near as he finds his favorite chair.
With a wave of his arm.
He beckons us near while whispering, a thankful prayer.
I have been waiting all day long, and now this time has come.
Walk. Skip, no, run, run, run
into his waiting arms.
His gentle hands, once covered in dirt,
now carefully washed away.
Tenderly, he holds our little hands as he says.
Let us play some music and sing a bit.
Daddy gently pulls us up close and folds
our small hands into his,
together we offer a heartfelt prayer to God, who always hears.
Then he tells us of his day and the people
or the animals that had demanded his time.

The stories he would tell, we could actually see in our mind.
As he would say, He had a story to tell,
but through the course of each
he would say we were always on his mind and in his heart.
We were at peace.
The world was tucked away.
There was no place, I would have rather
be at the end of every day.
My Daddy's hands are so capable and warm.
As we bid the day, good night,
In those hands, he reveals to us he loved us through it all,
all through the day.
And even through the night.

Laurie 2022

My Prayer for You

Today I pray you are blessed with someone,
to make your struggles more bearable.
Someone with a smile, with the ability to light up your day.
For we all need someone like that, from time to time,
to find Peace of Mind.
I pray you always find kind words rolling off your tongue,
instead of the judgment or criticism that could so easily
come, especially with some we meet along the way.
A word of praise for the one you see going through a bad time.
Think about it this way,
your voice may just be the best thing that they hear all day.
Or your smile could be the only smile
they see to brighten a dark day.
To appreciate the quiet moments where you can just
become still and breathe.
That is when you can gather your thoughts
for whatever may come next.
Something you may have been unable to foresee,
that will be in your path.
I pray you will always have the wisdom to distinguish
between what you are being offered,
compared to what you are truly worth.
These two things are never the same.
You are so much more,
than what you see looking back at you in the mirror,
each and every day.
That you see a reflection of love,
a sign from heaven that shows you just how special you are.
We need those now and again to realize we are not alone.
We might need that to remind us that our time is not yet done.
We are all still needed by someone,
and you are not alone.

Can that person be?
The one that we needed to meet.
To have genuine compassion for those who suffer
emotional or physical pain.
We all have needed a hand at times,
just to know we actually matter to someone.
That you keep a gentle heart, soft shoes.
May you find some flowers along the road,
a cool breeze or a warm fire to keep you cozy and comfortable.
May you be blessed with a thankful heart and a joyful spirit
each and every day.
With so much love to help you along the way
for these things,
I pray,
Amen

Laurie 2022

Winds Of Change

A strange wind is coming.
It is bringing a change.
As it gently blows across my face,
I feel all the unanswered questions beginning to fade away.
I do not remember them anymore.
Then I realized those answers never really mattered anyway.
A warm breeze touches my skin,
as I feel my soul beginning to awaken again.
To become alive as its awakening from a deep slumber,
reacting to this wind of change.
What I have been waiting an eternity for is here at last.
Now I am ready for this change, as never before.
I am ready for these winds of change.

Laurie 2022

It Is, What It Is

Never, never push the limits with someone
who uses the phrase
"It is,
What it is."
Those people are dangerous
simply because
they no longer allow circumstances
outside of their control
to affect their inner peace.
This person has successfully mastered
the art of acceptance.
Seeing the worst of life has changed them
to the point of accepting things and learning the lesson
to be learned.
They have learned, to just move on,
never looking back again.
They will not waste time standing and arguing with you.
Or disagreeing over something that should not matter.
This life to them,
is too short to waste time like that.
So, if you think you can manipulate them.
Bluff them, or threaten to leave them,
unless they comply with your demands.
I want you to realize this one true fact
and accept it for what it is,
for this is the brutal truth.
That they will never bow to an ideal,
for the sake of less conflict.
They may walk away,
or they may even hold the door for
you, as you walk away.
But either way,

you will be the one who will lose in the end,
because it is, what it is.
And that, my friend,
is the only truth
they live by.

Laurie 2022

One Day

I realized that the person looking back at me,
in the mirror that day was not the same person,
as I was on the inside.
There was a change in my life after that.
Nothing would ever be the same for me.
As I realized then,
that I did not even like that person in the mirror anymore,
if I was to be honest.
I really was not sure that I ever had.
That person looking back at me,
was the one, everyone else wanted me to be.
But who was I, without that influence?
I had no idea. None at all.
I had spent my whole life trying to be
perfect or as close as I could be.
Always looking for the best outfit or the ideal hairstyle,
that I thought would make someone else happy,
that would help me fit in.
To this world, that I had been born into.
Only to find, none of that ever really made any difference.
Not to me, not even to them.
Doing all the superficial things to try to please someone
that did not even matter.
Living that way for reasons that were not real,
in ways that were not really important.
Those things, never told my story, never showed who I could be.
I was never given the chance to find out.
The tale of failure and triumph.
Losing all in finding myself all over again,
but most of all, evolving my heart
and soul into the best person,
I could be.

Without a precast mold of what everyone else thought, I should be.
Looking in the mirror, I saw all my flaws,
my mistakes, all my failures.
And it was, I realized the image of someone who
could never be perfect, or ever wanted to be.
But that was the beauty of it all, I did not have to be.
Moreover, I had no desire to be perfect or fit in with the crowd,
or to be like everyone else.
I did not want to be anyone but me.
Show me the real ones.
The people are full of flaws, scars, and scratches.
The broken hearts with hands full of
matches, to burn it all down.
The brutally honest souls, who tell it like it is.
They may have nothing of their own but
would always have your back.
Strive to be the one who will have theirs, if need be.
You can always count on those people, to be real.
Not to be someone who would take
you apart, behind your back,
when they are upset or unhappy,
with something you might have done.
Or make sure that all know,
how much they may have done for you,
trying to make themselves look better
by tearing you down.
I never want to be that miserable,
someone who would strive to blame someone else,
for my own inadequate self.
That brutally honest and loyal person
is who I strive to be each and every day.
The one who has your back no matter what.
I realize now that time will cause beauty to fade
and time may wrinkle, my less than perfect skin
as it will also change my body.

Even my energy and drive at some point,
but my heart and soul, those amazing parts of myself that I value,
will keep growing and making a difference to all around me.
Getting better and better each day.
So, I have stopped trying to be trendy, cool, and hip.
Stylish is not even a word I use.
Much more unique is my goal.
I am working on being authentic, caring and kind.
I want to be the one who can be counted
on when you are in a bind.
I may not have much money, but I can make sure
you never go without one way or another.
The world needs more of that.
I need more of that in my own life.
I am letting go of the things I cannot change.
And focusing more on what I can.
In the end, what matters most is my peace of mind.
Maybe happiness is fleeting, but I can still have a good life,
to be content with my own life, within my world and happy
working on things around me, helping
someone else when I can.
I cannot control where my path leads me.
Or where tomorrow brings me.
But I can control how I let it affect me, rain, or shine,
whether hot or cold, stormy, or calm,
I always keep moving forward and doing the thing
as I know is right.
If you ask me a question, be prepared for the answer.
This life is a surprisingly good place to
be, to have the peace of mind.
In knowing that I have tried to be all,
that I can be,
that is enough for me.

Laurie 2022

In Life

One day I awoke, and my world had changed.
I see God's great portrait now.
It is not the same.
I gazed out the window through new eyes,
like the eyes of a young child, never
seeing this world looking so wild.
All of God's creation now comes into light.
Oh, how I wish you could see this as
my eyes do, this grand sight.
The trees I now see, like never before.
As I watched,
they dropped their leaves to lay upon the earth's floor.
The moon, the sun, and the stars.
The wild winds and the driving rain, even the sage,
will never be the same.
I see the lavender as it blows wildly.
I smell the spice upon the wind.
Is this what it is like for us to grow old,
to feel an old soul, to never be young again?
I watch as the frightened people scurry about
with their hearts filled with fear, their minds filled with doubt.
Too busy to give a neighbor a second thought?
Or even a kind hello?
I guess that could have been me, just a short time ago.
Time passes like water, flowing over and over through time,
passing us all, never to return that same way again.
Soften your heart and let your eyes learn.
Waste not one minute of this life.
Miss not the special moments,
all the great mysteries like a songbird in flight.
Wake in the morning
with a prayer in your heart and a bounce in your step,

so that one day we might look at this world, with an open heart
and see what God has made in all his glory.
We can rejoice and see all the blessings that is ours to keep.
All there is in life for us to see.

Laurie, 2021

Only Time

I will never proclaim to be anyone special,
or anywhere near, to perfect,
but I do protect my peace at all costs.
If you threaten my peace,
I will wish you well and send you on your way.
I do not have the time to rebuild myself over and over again,
day after day.
You see, I fight for my peace quietly in so many different ways.
There was a point in my life,
when I did not wake up in peace,
I would very seldom go to sleep in peace.
I would crawl there, and sometimes
just knowing I was still alive, was enough.
It was enough to have faith, that I would get there in time.
There is no reason for anyone
who cares about me, to steal my peace.
And if they do?
Well, I do not have the time nor the energy
to explain to them,
who I am.
If they did not hear me the first time,
they likely will never hear me again.
I roam in a frequency, heard by few.
I take time to create my peace, finding my way back to myself
many times, over
in many different ways.
As so many broken ones will do,
these many broken trails, will keep taking me towards home.
I am still learning that chaos is not my home.
I am still letting this war for peace,
trickle through and out of my veins.
I can feel it.

I am almost there.
I am always, almost there.
I gave myself time to heal. Time to think.
Time to recover and relax my mind.
Time to love my life again.
And time to just learn to be alone.
Well, it gave me more time.
Gave me time to love myself again.
To find another like me.
Time to live again,
for time
Is only time.

Laurie 2022

My life

My life is just a reflection.
Nothing is anymore, like the lights on the water,
flickering in my imagination, as I set here on the shore.
I gaze across the water to see what has been
or might have been,
but the image is distorted
as the surface of the water, is ripples in the wind.
Not long ago I could feel, what I could not see.
Today things are double, but which one could it be?
The reflection in the mirror, is that of someone old
with a face of wrinkles and eyes, which
have grown dim with age.
I wait for the lake to calm, to be still and smooth again
for me to see my reflection upon its surface.
So maybe I can see the past in my mind.
To soothe my heart, look past my eyes.
The days of youth are still fairly clear,
but my thoughts leave lately,
robbing me of what was so dear.
Ideas, I cast like a rock into the lake.
They sink to the bottom, and only ripples of them remain.
The ripples are strong,
as I once had been in my own unique way.
But as time carries them out there, there is not much left to say.
I find myself standing at the water's edge, thinking
of those, to whom I had made a pledge.
My heart is sinking, but my mind fights to stay,
a process that I cannot slow down, much less master
And I cannot make it go away.
So, I must accept what is happening and enjoy this day,
holding on to the memories until they fade away,
as I know they soon will.

So, as I sit and think,
watching the sun slowly sinking into the west.
I realize all that really matters.
I still have.
That reflected image in the water,
is of someone who has lived a life to the fullest
and still many more lives, to live.
A life rich with memories and wisdom to share.
Loved ones still waiting, for the smile.
That sparkle and wit which age can never dull.
I realized all that matters,
I still have.

Laurie 2022

My Mother

She is the one that everyone depends on.
The woman that always appears
to get it all done.
With a smile that brightens a dark day,
with ease she conquers the fears.
Helping all around her, never refusing a call.
All the while, with a smile on her face and a pep in her step.
They never know what hides, behind those bright blue eyes.
She does not ask for help.
Even when she falters, or even when she slows down.
But what the others never seemed to notice,
is that she has her moments too.
She has the tears and the fears of not being enough,
but there is no one else that steps up and takes the load
when she is tired of being the strong one.
Carrying the weight of the world, to
keep it from your shoulders
and being there for everyone else who needs her,
she lies in bed at night more times than not,
thinking more than she is sleeping.
Wondering how she is going to get it all done?
But that is the beautiful thing, about a strong woman.
She always finds a way, even though her soul is weary,
and her heart is so bone tired at times.
Sometimes she just wishes
she could fall into someone else's arms
and just be,
just a rest in the quiet, if only for a night.
But she just has that thought, for just a moment.
Do not misunderstand, she loves her
life and being the strong one.
But sometimes,

Sometimes she just does not want to be that one,
that everyone else looks to.
To solve their problems or to lift them up.
To help things get done, she did not
choose her life, it chose her.
She was never given a chance.
She was created this way as few
are, and many never know
the blessing of having a woman
like her, until she is gone.
Failure after heartbreak.
Disaster after disappointment,
she forged her strengths, from each lesson she learned.
And in these fires of her struggles, she has grown.
So, as she lies in bed, staring at the ceiling,
a solitary tear creeps down her cheek.
There is such emotion and raw feeling,
all woven into that solitary teardrop rolling down her face.
Anxiety, worry, concern and care for her loved ones.
All these sentiments, that she is learned
to channel into courage,
into the bravery and strength, that which
makes her seem unstoppable.
She was never given a choice, and she is okay with that,
but sometimes she wishes she could rest her weary soul.
That is when the thoughts, of the beautiful parts of her life
flood into her mind and she smiles,
Wiping away the tears with a deep breath.
She will stand to face a new day.
She would not trade her life for anything,
because there is so much love and joy in her days.
Maybe they don't notice when she falters, and
perhaps no one sees, when she's tired.
But they do not have to.
Her warrior's heart and fighting spirit,

keep her pushing forward.
She will rest later today.
Like all the other days.
She is going to be unstoppable.

Laurie 2022

Secret To Life

Sitting here thinking
as the steam rolls up from the surface of a hot cup of coffee.
Curling and winding, like the rolling thoughts in my mind.
I am in a thinking mood this morning,
as most days it seems.
Thinking back and remembering,
thinking about all the people
who have come into my life.
Although, some of them leave my life too early.
Or too early for me, it may seem.
Maybe some, that I thought, would never leave,
I had hoped they were meant to stay forever.
A loved one that was supposed to have always been there,
such a crucial and important part of my life.
When we give our love; we give all of ourselves.
We give of everything we have to offer,
yet in the end, they may still have to go.
Even though we feel like it was not enough at the time,
or that we gave more to them and that it was not returned,
in the way we thought it should have been.
Yet how many times in our lives have we taken from others
without a thought of repayment?
Sometimes, not even a simple thank you, as if we forgot.
We just knew, they would understand.
But then receive that from another, did we understand?
What we should have given to someone before, now we see?
But without first taking a moment to think,
of their expectations, we never know.
Most times, as we humans tend to forget
someone else's feelings, never realizing, it may
seem or feel like taking to them also.

As it was the dominant need at the moment, foremost in your
mind, you may never have given it a conscious thought.
But in that moment, it does not feel that
way, when it happens to you.
Sometimes we simply forget
that we all have taken, or all we have received before, without
taking the time to say thank you or something in kind.
Because when we give with expectations of a return,
for accolades, adorations, or praise of some sort
we should have never given to begin with.
That is not a gift of yourself to another.
That is a loan or a bribe that a return in kind, is expected for.
Perhaps, this is why
Relationships, Friendships and Families
break down.
Perhaps this is the reason people,
who were supposed to stay in our lives and never leave,
leave way too soon.
Perhaps a heartfelt "Thank you" or a simple "I appreciate you"
is not what we thought we deserved.
Have we nullified the effort they made?
The small things that were done, in an
attempt to return that gift?
In their own ways, what we received in our way of thinking
was not as glamorous or loud enough,
to make the world see us?
For everyone to see that we were such
a generous giver, this time.
Yet maybe it was all that that person had to give,
at that moment in their lives.
Just maybe it was all they had; all they had left and
was a sacrifice, we should have appreciated more.
And yet it will never be enough.
For the one who always expects something more, in return.
All through life, we see givers or takers in all points and times.

They are both, possibly all at the same time.
Most times we give more than we think, we have received.
And at other times we know receive more,
than we could ever have hoped or dreamed,
or could ever be thankful enough for.
The wonderful thing is
that no matter what we give or how much we give.
It is always returned to us in some way or another
and so unexpectedly at times.
Not always the way we wanted it, but it is always paid back.
That is, if we choose to see it,
maybe in the small moments we miss,
but sometimes not until they are gone.
Maybe, maybe small gestures or advice, a hug on a tough day.
As we sit here, in the evenings, now alone
as we think back, to so many corners hidden in our mind.
We try to hold these memories closer now.
As we sit in the quiet, we find more and more, sifting through
our memories of all the forgotten moments or blessings.
The moments of someone's time, we receive in payment
are the things, we can never forget.
What we receive back from life is priceless, though
we may choose not to see it at the time.
The attitude that we have about giving and
receiving is what our legacy will read.
The willingness to go that extra mile or stay an extra hour
or make that extra plate, for someone who is alone.
These small things will never be forgotten,
at the end of a hard day.
But the expectations we may or may not
have set before we reach out,
should reflect the path, we walk along the way also.
I am slowly starting to understand, so many things
that had broken my heart.
Things I had never understood until now.

Many may have been gifts, that I was yet to understand.
That to me
may very well be the secret of life.
Such as it is.

Laurie 2021

Reflections

I am sometimes guilty, every so often
Of pausing for just a moment to reflect.
Of thinking upon the many reasons,
I may have made certain decisions, for my life.
As I sat wondering this and pondering why?
I ask myself why I would have done
this or that, until that perfect moment in time,
when the time was right.
Deep within the forest walking, I moved along that trail for a bit,
till I was standing on the lakeshore.
The answers began to come to me in the silence.
One by one, as if in a timed sequence,
just like it is or what it was supposed to be.
As I set comfortably now, reveling in the solitude of nature
on a beach of finely sifted sand and rocks.
Here I sat, as still as still could be,
listening so quietly and carefully.
I realized that what may seem at times,
have been quite unclear, suddenly changing
my mind here and there.
As I felt myself shifting to a clearer understanding
of what I had been seeking all this time,
during my walk through the forest this day.
I seemed to have acquired my answers,
I had been trying to find.
I then noticed, as I quickly contemplated the answers to life.
That the lake surface has slowly changed.
It is now clearly and wisely reflecting its truth.
As I soon began to realize,
My answers appear now to be crystal clear as well.
With my newly acquired peace of mind.
Reflections,

just like the waters of the lake,
now seem to be reflecting back to me.
My life and mind, no longer chaos now
Life had put me exactly where; I had needed too be.

Laurie 2022

Right Now

Hey, you over there scrolling through your phone right now.
I know that you are busy
and the world requires a lot of your attention.
But before you take another step further today,
I need you to stop and do something for me.
I need you to stop right here,
right where you are.
I need you to look at this world around you.
I need you to really take a look,
at whatever people might be surrounding you.
I need you to notice the light.
As its falling upon you, I need you to notice
because this is your life.
This is your day.
It may look differently than you expected
right now, but just wait.
It may be exceptionally hard right now, but it won't last forever.
Or it may be better than you ever thought possible right now.
But it is still your life right now, in this very moment.
And at this moment in time, in this very spot,
is where anything can happen.
Right now, is where Magic can be created.
When you finally make that phone call, write that letter,
or reach out that hand.
Right now, is where peace can be sought.
When we say, "I am sorry," or "I forgive you."
Even, "Let us move forward."
Right now, is where that freedom can be found.
When you finally decide that the punishment is over
and you whisper to yourself,
"I am allowed to be happy right now."
This truth alters lives, heals hearts, and builds dreams.

Notice it,
because you are making a choice about what to do with it.
Right now
this moment is what you have been waiting for.
It is happening right before your very eyes,
and in this moment, is all that we have.
So, when I say that I need you to do something for me.
What I am really saying,
is that I need you to realize something for yourself.
Right now
This moment can change everything about
you and your life as you know it now.
So let it.
Right now

Laurie 2022

Someone Is Waiting

Somewhere, there is someone thinking of you.
Someone is so immensely proud of you.
Someone is thinking of you. Someone, caring about you.
Somewhere, someone misses you.
Someone wants to have a day, just to sit and talk to you.
Someone, wants to be with you on those hard days,
praying and holding hopes you are not in trouble.
Someone is thankful for the support you have
provided to them, on their hard days.
Someone, wants to be there to hold your hand,
as you held theirs.
Someone hopes everything turns out all right for you.
Someone wants you to be happy.
Someone wants you to find him or her, they are waiting.
Someone is celebrating your successes,
as they would their own.
Someone thinks that you are a gift to this harsh world.
Someone hopes you are not too cold or too hot.
Someone wants to hug you or even loves you.
Someone is admiring your strength.
Someone is thinking of you and smiling.
Someone wants to be at your shoulder, for you to lean on.
Someone wants to go out with you and share the day.
To share the smiles with you, that only with you, they can.
Someone thinks the world of you.
They want to protect you and will do anything for you.
Someone prays to be forgiven.
Someone is grateful for your forgiveness.
Someone wants to laugh with you.
Wants to Remember, the good days
And wishes that you were there,
remembering all that you did.

All the different little ways, which was so perfect.
Someone is thanking God for you, right now.
And they need to know that your love is unconditional.
Someone values your advice.
Someone, wants to know you are on your way home
And they want to tell you how much they care.
Someone wants to share their dreams with you.
And the rest of your life.
Someone, wants to hold you in their heart,
wants you to hold them in your heart, while treasuring
that wild spirit as it is,
never wanting you to change
Someone wishes they could stop time, just because of you.
Someone, thanks God, for your friendship and love
and cannot wait to see you again
Someone, loves you, for just who you are.
Loves the way you make them feel.
Even the blunt honesty and all, even with its sting at times.
Someone, wants to be with you, for the rest of their days,
wants to know that you are there for them, the same way.
Someone is so glad that you are his or her friend.
Someone, stayed up all night
just thinking about you, wondering if you are all right
Someone. is alive today because of you.
Someone is wishing that you had noticed, him or her.
Someone wants to get to know you better.
Someone wants to be near you and misses your smile.
Just to be close, for just a little while
And has so much faith in your wisdom and advice.
Someone needs you to send them this letter.
Maybe needs your support?
Needs that faith that you have in them.
Someone will cry when they read this.
Someone, hears a song

that reminds them of you and picks up the phone to call
before realizing you are gone.
Someone is there.
Waiting.

Laurie 2022

Safe

They say that the scars that hurt the most
are what defines our heart and lives, makes us who we are.
And you are only human if you have made mistakes.
But the art of correcting those mistakes, is what makes us grow.
As an individual into our own person,
they speak and grow, by letting things go.
That is a form of just giving up and not even trying.
Who makes these rules anyway?
Then they want you to play it safe,
play it safe??!!
What does that even mean??
That when you have the world in the palm of your hand,
yet you let it go??
Do you stand and watch as it crumbles and falls apart?
Then you blame it on fate, blame it on circumstances,
blame it on bad advice?
Anything to ease that pain and explain
away why you did not see.
You did not see, what you held within your grasp?
Not until it was already gone, playing it
safe as you had been advised?
You chased the shadows and the memories,
trying to hide from the truth.
And yet you know, even as you played it safe,
as you were told to do, you know what you threw away.
And yet.
You played it safe, as you had been told.
Some say when it rains it pours.
Some days you will still look at the clouds and ask why?
Many years of no one there to answer
to speak the word's, you so desperately needed to hear.
But you played it safe, didn't you?

That is why you are here.
Will you play it safe and forget to live a life?
I truly hope you do not.
There is so much more to experience and see out there.
Even though we may feel our heart breaking, we will live.
Through betrayal deeper than we even could think,
we could bear in that moment.
As we play it safe.
We will find so many that need that soft voice or touch,
just to make it through their days.
Sometimes that voice of encouragement or compassion,
it may be the only voice they hear.
Always remember if you always play it safe,
you will lose a chance at living a life.
Always on the guard against hurt,
they may never find their way
to your heart, if you play it safe.

Laurie 2022

As She Was Born to Be

She has learned the hard way.
No one was coming to save her.
She could not depend on anyone else
having fought the hard battles, been knocked down
more times than she could count,
and somehow, she always managed to get up one more
time, managing to find a way to keep moving.
She was determined to survive.
No,
not to just survive, but to live.
Help was not coming,
back up never happened.
Someone to rescue her?
Not without costing more than her soul, could pay.
She never had any of those things.
So, she stopped looking for a knight in shining armor
and started looking for her sword.
That knight in shining armor.
Generally turned out to be a majestic mistake.
Wrapped in tinfoil, usually generic tinfoil, at that.
She found that she did not need to be saved, rescued, or fixed.
She just needed to do, what she did best.
Keep going, keep pushing forward, keep smiling,
and kept rising as she moved up that mountain.
No, it was not easy.
There were days, weeks, and years that she wanted to quit,
throw in the towel and give in ...
But that was not who she was or who she would ever be.
She would only fail, only if she refused to keep trying.
Her strength, grace, and courage
were all forged in those same coals
that had once tried to burn her down.
Not only, did she keep going,

she would emerge from the flames burnished brighter.
Brighter and much stronger, than what and who,
had tried to burn her down.
She has been taught her inner strength here,
more than an easier path, could ever have taught her.
She reminded herself often, that she was strong
because of the trials.
And she could overcome anything if she kept fighting.
So, she did.
Through the heartbreak and the disappointments,
even the anguish of loss.
From saying goodbye to people, she had
never dreamed would walk away.
Some she would never have let go had she been given a choice,
they just weren't meant to linger any longer in this life.
She had always believed the ones meant for her,
would always find a way to stay in her life.
So, she taught herself to let the others go.
Continuing to hold those beautiful souls tightly, that stayed.
And love?
What is that really?
She would just smile at the men,
full of their own ego and bravado and she would move on.
They were not there for her for who she was.
They just needed a boost to their ego.
She was just a challenge, as she seemed to be so distant
and far from approachable, so she never wasted her time.
She would wait for the one who would be there
without expectation or demands.
Who was her equal and would love, who she was now.
She needed someone to stand beside her, as her equal.
Not to try and tame her or change her.
Constantly reminding her, of how much they had given
or done.
Always expecting something in return.

You see, she did not need a man to make
her whole or keep her in life.
She was already happy and complete just the way she was.
She knew how to fight her own battles, make her own choices,
She just needed someone to love her
the way she loved her people, she had
gathered close to her heart.
And anyone that wanted to win her heart,
they did not need to bring a sword, armor, or glorious words.
They just needed to be real. to be honest
and as she was to them.
To keep their word, to stand their ground and to be steadfast,
to be someone she could trust, even when her back was turned.
In her story, she did not need a hero,
and that is exactly how she planned to keep it.
She had been forged in the flames and was strong enough
to stand alone.
She smiled at the challenges and stepped over them
as if to say "Not today, Satan" as she walked along
and went about her days.
Until the day, she finds that one
that is strong enough to stand beside her.
Until then, she will keep living life fully,
loving her people passionately and rising high
like she was meant to do,
always there when needed.
Or helping someone else stand
for there, she is happy
just the way she was meant to be.
And in the end, that is what matters the most.
Her happily ever after started and ended
the way it was supposed to, with her.
Strong, independent, and free
as she was born to be.

Laurie 2022

The Strong Woman

She is not one, that will ever tell you
She has it all figured out.
That will never be a statement, you will hear from her.
She may run back and forth through most of her days
without a clue of anyone else's reality.
Not a clue of how she will get it all done,
make it all work,
or even where to find all the answers
she is looking for.
She does not know how she will pay all the bills for the month,
or even how to just stand still and breathe some days.
But that is just the thing about a strong,
independent, resourceful, headstrong woman.
She will never worry about the how,
for she will always say, I will figure it out.
And she will do exactly as she says,
given a bit of time to think.
That is just who she is.
And how she has stamina and determination
and stubbornness that her life has taught
her, you may never understand.
She was never given any idea of who she would become,
how she would make her life work, why it was the way it is.
There has never been the easy path or help along the journey.
Someone to ease the way for her, if she
would have even let them.
She had to learn, to depend upon herself for support
to take care of her loved ones,
and that has made all the difference to her.
She will tell you if you are brave enough to ask her.
But with her blunt honesty, beware.
You may not like her answer, but it will be the truth, either way.

She makes mistakes all the time, trips
and falls a time or two a day.
In her own mind, she has been a horrible human at times.
Made horrible decisions and worse mistakes, but she
always manages to find her way to better days.
So, when she climbs to the top of the mountain
she has been forced to overcome.
She does so with pride
and a fierce sense of accomplishment.
Independence in her demeanor and triumph in her eyes,
she arrives, as a pure force of nature.
She did it even when she thought she could not,
even when everyone else expected her to fall
and would need to be picked back up.
She picked and beat the odds, fought back, and rose higher.
More times, than anyone could have imagined possible.
That is how she knows.
She always knows, with her own ingenuity and prayer,
anything is possible.
But only if she sets her mind to it.
The only one who can defeat her is herself.
Her own doubts, her own fears, her own lack of focus.
Or simply, just not trying hard enough but
that is just not going to happen.
Not in her story.
She will turn that page, start a brand-new chapter,
before she allows that to happen again.
She will create a new beginning,
which in turn will change the ending.
Over and over and over again until she gets it right.
That is just what she does.
But you can rest assured, she will never stay down,
quit, or stop trying.
You will never be able to say she quit or
just simply gave in to defeat.

For each and every time she fell down, she got up one time
more than she fell.
She is stronger and harder than she probably has to be.
That one that never gives up, not ever.
You will see she will find a way.
Maybe not the way she planned at first, but she
will always find a way to make it work.
So, if you see her on her knees battling life
and struggling to survive, do not worry.
Be prepared to watch her rise, from the ashes of that fire.
For as a phoenix from the fables and
folklore, she will keep rising
until she shows, rising in the flames.
She keeps showing up, keeps trying, keeps moving forward.
Even moving slowly, is still progress.
She forged her strength in those fires,
that would have consumed anyone else.
But they made her, as she is, an indestructible force.
The fires, well, they just made her stronger,
more resilient, more adaptable in a crisis.
A hard-to-understand place in life.
So, when I tell you that she is one-of-a-kind, make no mistake,
You will never find another like her.
Appreciate her like she deserves.
Women like her do not come along very often.
Many burn out before their time, saving others dear to them.
She is amazing, just the way that she is.
Do not ever make the mistake of trying to change that.
If she gives up that part of her, there
is nothing left of who she is.
She is the force of life, of nature.
She is a perfect storm.
So, if you are ever lucky enough to be pulled into
her circle of life, treasure that and let her be.
Let her live, as she was meant to be,

life will never be boring,
for she is a perfectly,
imperfect storm.
Take a look into the mirror and appreciate what you see,
who you can be.
For this
is who you are.

Laurie 2022

Little Things

Restless and wild, in a unique chaotic kind of natural beauty.
A feather dancing in the wind, you cannot help but admire.
Her strength fascinates you, as you watch her lean into the fall,
way too far out over the edge.
Looking at her even now, you seem to see no fear at all.
The wind beneath her wings lifts her high.
She is a lady in and above all things.
Her grace and beauty surrounds wherever she may go.
Her life touches all that is around her.
If you are lucky enough to be in her life, love will abound.
But some days, her pain she will wear as a badge of honor.
Yet you will never know,
She spent years earning her place in life,
creating a peace around, for all who hold her close.
She is the calm, in the midst of a chaotic day.
But make no mistake, she can also be the chaos in the storm,
interrupting the calm day too.
You may know her for years, but never knowing the answer
to the mystery
that makes her who she is.
Many are attracted to the beam of light she radiates.
But few will be brave enough to stay.
As she has a way of dignity and grace
that can intimidate some,
without meaning to be that way.
Her carriage, her attitudes toward life, her sheer
determination to overcome and conquer all in her path.
She has mastered this as a habit, an oath to live by.
All of this makes her a treasure sought by many.
But will be cherished by one.
She will be the one, who will have a soul mate for life
if he is brave enough to fight for her hand.

It will not be an easy victory.
For he will need to comprehend, she will never need him,
to complete her or to make her way in life.
But just for who they are as one, for a companion
with whom she can spend her time.
Someone to cherish in those small ways,
in ways that only that she can.
She will never be swayed, for money or for things,
but for the little moments a special heart
will be adding to her life.
For those little things, to some.
Are what matters to her the most.

Laurie, 2022

Failure Will Never Be

She never knew, that when people met her,
that they would marvel at her strength and resilience.
They seemed to think that she was just born that way
that everything just came easy.
She made struggles and chaos look easy,
almost effortless to them.
They would see her struggle sometimes,
but she never seemed to give in.
But the longer they knew her,
came the knowledge that she would never quit.
Failure was just not in her repertoire, and that was okay.
They were welcome to think, what they wanted,
because that is just the way it is, and they would
have drawn their own opinions anyway.
No one, but her closest friends and family
knew about her journey,
and that is the way she wanted it to be.
She quietly laid her foundations, finished her projects,
and built a life, behind her screen of privacy.
This world did not need to know, the price she had paid
to become the force of nature she is now.
The years, she paid in tears or the miles she traveled alone,
to get where she is now.
Her sacrifices.
Her failures and setbacks
were ever meant to be on display.
Never necessary for the public to know or ever needed
for them to have formed an opinion of her.
But they are still part of her story.
Her narrative is the tale of growth,
from a broken young woman learning to survive.
To building a new life, without asking for help from anyone,

except those close enough to keep her story to themselves.
Those who understood, her privacy was utmost.
She did not become bitter, by the rejections or disappointments.
Or from the struggles she survived, to achieve her dreams,
the failures and the do overs.
Time after time she became better, she did not settle for less.
She followed the dreams, sometimes the long way around
or in an unconventional method, it would seem to some.
But she did follow through and thrived.
Each day she learned a little more, grew a little bit stronger,
and fought a little harder for her dreams.
She did not ask for pity, help or sympathy.
Recognition was never the goal.
Just to be better than she was, the day before.
Through each and every day afterwards,
she just found a way to always get it done.
And one day, that same little girl looked in the mirror
and realized that she had become a strong mature woman.
A warrior in fact, who was capable of so much more
than anyone ever believed she could do or go so much farther,
than believed possible by most.
That she has gone so far, from where she started from,
was always a mystery to many.
She smiled that quiet, careful smile in that moment
because she knew, but never spoke.
That she had earned every bit of who she was
and who she had become.
And the ones who wanted to doubt her?
Well,
those people did not really matter much anyway.
She would just lower her gaze, with that smile and
invite them to walk through the fire with her,
as if they would dare.
She had learned long ago how to walk through
and emerge tougher and unscathed.

So, she just did what she always had done.
Keep going. Kept fighting. Kept climbing.
One step after another.
She would walk past the disrespect and dismissal of others
and keep rising.
She still had a life to conquer,
and she was not going to let anyone, or anything,
stand in her way.
Success with character.
Victory with respect.
Happiness with heart.
Maybe she couldn't change the world,
but she knew she could always change her world.
And she did.
Along with the world around her,
for others she had adopted into her world.
She surrounded herself
with the people who mattered most to her.
And in her circle of loyalty,
these precious ones, she kept close.
That is all that mattered to her, in her life.
How do I know this little girl now,
all grown up,
the strong warrior I, see?
She is me, and I am still rising,
still learning, still moving forward
Without ever having a desire to quit.
I realize now that we can only fail,
if we quit or do not get up,
when we fall.
I have no intention of failing.
Failure is no longer a part of my vocabulary.
Nor will it ever,
Be a part of my future

Laurie 2022

Just The Way She Was

She was not a woman,
that people
could easily understand.
They could not comprehend her reasoning
and logic for most situations.
It was not for their lack of trying though.
She just did not make sense to them.
To her, it was easy, it was only plain common sense to her.
She was always kind and smiling,
but she never really let her guard down.
Did not trust quickly, and she had her reasons.
Her eyes alone could speak volumes
about who she truly was.
But most never bothered to look past her looks, to see
past the smile that never quite reaches her eyes.
Taking time to uncover her true depths.
She had a mind of her own, a simple way of thinking
that would leave most behind wondering,
what had just happened.
Truthfully, she was a unique one,
and she protected who she was and her privacy
with a quiet ferocity, as she did her loved ones.
Saving her real beauty for her special ones,
the people that took time to figure her out,
that knew her on a different level.
An intimate level, her loved ones understood her.
Those were her people.
The people she loved, were much like her.
With old souls, empathetic spirits
that could read others in ways,
that intimidated the ones, who could not.

Most could not understand, these odd
people, that were so content
just being.
They possessed wisdom beyond their years and a love deeper
than the world understood.
The version of what most needed in their life
to be complete but never patient enough to find.
Like them, she needed more than a common love, a
mediocre attachment, or a surface relationship.
For when she loved, she gave her all,
expecting the same in return.
If she could not give her all to someone
or to anything she was doing,
In life, she walked away.
She did not know how to do anything
halfway, including love or friendships.
She knew she was not for everyone to understand.
There would always be people,
that wanted to capture who she was or wanted to love her.
But they did not really know how.
Those were the ones, who tried to love her on their terms.
While expecting her to change for them.
Without ever truly trying to unravel her mystery
or taking the time, to engage her mind.
That was normal she supposed, as she
had been told many times before.
So, she thought nothing of it and moved on.
The world was full of ordinary people, leading normal lives
with average dreams.
Never looking for the extraordinary, in anything.
Never knowing that desire to find more and
discover all that is to be found.
She swore never to walk that path.
It just was not for her.
She needed so much more than an ordinary life.

Her heart and mind yearned
for the most intimate relationships
and the contentment of an uncommon love.
Both for herself and others around her.
And she relentlessly pursued this, as in
what mattered most to her.
She did not try to be different; she just
was and always had been.
Her soul was distinctly rich, her mind
was wired differently than most, never seemed to
slow down, always seeking more knowledge.
She was never found to be following the easier path
as if she had never seen a different road.
Honestly, she could not tell you why
she was so deeply passionate about life.
Only that her heart and soul would not let her be any other way.
She would shy away from the spotlights she had known
and instead
would revel in the brilliant allure of the stars,
or in the rising of a moon.
Or a wild thunderstorm with lightning and wind.
You would often find her soaking in
a beautiful sunrise
or losing herself in the fading rays
of a richly hued sunset.
She knew who she was,
even as she could not really explain it at times.
She was an old soul.
Caught somewhere between a strong mind and a fragile heart.
But most of all, she was happy in her life, heart, and soul.
She was unforgettable as a unique one and she was loved.
She was truly content
to be just the way she was.

Laurie 2022

Strengths

She was the one with a huge heart.
Doling out love, without ever expecting it in return,
She loved intensely, for she found joy in it
without any expectations.
She was not naive or blind, or simple minded by any means.
She just always believed in the inherent good of people.
She gave everyone the benefit of the doubt,
even when they turned their backs on her
and tore her heart in pieces.
Deep down, she knew the risk, but she refused to become jaded
or change how she lived and loved.
Time and again she'd kissed a frog,
hoping he had become a Prince,
only to find out his ugly truths, the hard way.
For instead of a frog, she had found a wart covered old toad.
But that did not change who she was or how she lived.
She would always listen to her heart.
She would still pursue passion fiercely.
She forgave when she knew she should not.
She loved fully in spite of the risk,
and she never turned her back
on the people she loved,
regardless of how often she had gotten hurt.
She gave them chance upon chance,
believing they were good people
until they ultimately proved they weren't.
But when she was done with someone, she was utterly done.
No more chances.
Forgiveness, or one more tries, she was just done.
But she gave her whole heart, to the ones that stayed?
They were her heart, and she would do anything for them.
Even the ones, who burned holes in her heart

as she was trying to love them.
She let them go and never looked back again.
It hurt her heart to know, that she had poured
every bit of love and compassion into those people,
but they never treated her the same.
So, she let them go and walked away.
She knew love was a fiery chance, burning her to the ground
as much as it would spark her passions and desires.
She just did not care.
She was strong enough to pick up the pieces
and knew that finding her future love
would take effort and courage.
So that is just what she did.
She followed her heart and loved hard when she could.
And if she got hurt?
She picked up the pieces
and moved on without ever slowing down.
She was determined to find her love story
and kept leaping into the flames.
She knew that sooner or later.
she would find the one worth
being burned for.
Until then?
She would live fully and keep going.
Strong, beautiful, independent, and free.

Laurie 2022

Just To Be Free

She always had her own way about her,
an odd way of doing things
and a unique style when living her life.
She is not the usual or ordinary.
She's far from that, not a woman that fits
into any stereotype or pattern,
or a precast mold.
Because that is what made her happy
and brought her peace,
in being different.
The rebel in the mix.
Truthfully, most of the people that she met
did not understand her at all.
They thought she was too focused or intense,
maybe stuck up,
or too independent or untouchable.
And because of that, most have alienated her,
out of fear of the unknown.
Not that it bothered her that much.
Most would rather embrace
the usual confines
of their comfort zones.
Rather than step out into the unknown,
that different world, that she represented.
She has a beautiful way about her,
true to who she is and unstoppable,
once she gets an idea in her mind.
With an undying loyalty
to all who she calls her own.
Uncompromising in her character, she will stand true to herself.
Her words are her bond, with no compromise.
It is either black or white.

With her, no gray zones can be found.
She stands for what she believes in
and follows her heart
almost to a fault sometimes.
Her brutal honesty carries a sharp bite at times,
but never intentionally meaning to hurt, those she loves.
She is not afraid to put herself out there
and risk all of her heart.
To chase her dreams and desires.
She is never going to be the one living for tomorrow,
and playing it safe.
Today is where her dreams lay,
to carry her into tomorrow.
She is a wild one, unafraid to do the unthinkable,
to be herself and to be free.
It has taken most of her lifetime, to find out who she is.
She now has no intention, of ever going back to that person.
Maybe she'll take a trip, without a destination.
Maybe she'll start a new business, build more on
her projects, or make more garden spots.
She will dance outside in the rain, when it begins to storm,
thunder and lightning booming and flashing across the sky
all through the wild, windy nights.
She will go somewhere; she's never been before.
Just to see where she ends up.
Try a new hobby or a new career,
she has never tried before.
All for experiencing the people, places, and dreams
she will find all along the way.
She is free in that way, in that most will never understand
or be brave enough to ever try.
But she is more than okay, with that.
It makes her who she is.
It is her contentment, living her best life,
and being an authentic person.

That is who she strives to be.
There is a lot of great people, doing amazing things out there,
in this life, to be sure.
But once you meet her, you may never forget her.
For she is more than just a person, a pretty
face, or an interesting character.
She has a knack for carving herself, a place in your heart
and that feeling of belonging.
She just stays right there with you.
She is a brave and a passionate spirit,
who if given half the chance
she will and can change your life
if or when you are ready to let go of who you are
and who you think you should be.
When you are ready to embrace who you might become,
or you are not afraid to take a chance for her,
that is who she will be.
Fiery, unique, independent, and challenging to understand or
Nearly impossible to keep up with,
just the way she always wanted to be.
Different and unashamedly broken.
She will never settle for less, than all.
She will continue learning and growing, till her days are gone.
For she has many things to learn, to see, to complete
before that time comes.
If you stay close, bored you would never be.
For if you can keep pace with her,
you might understand what she means.
When she says
she only wants to be free.

Laurie 2022

Every Day

Slow me down.
Lord,
calm the sound of my heart.
Be the quieting in my mind.
Steady my hurried pace with the visions,
in your eternal span of time.
Give me patience through the confusion of my days,
a touch of calm and calmness
in the beauty of silence.
In the soothing music of the cool, clear waters,
all that lives in my memories,
through the magical powers of my dreams.
Teach me the art of slowing down, to
savor the touch of a flower,
to chat with an old friend or make a new one.
To enjoy each new day.
Taking the time to watch a spider build her web
or to see the clouds.
To sing a few lines of a favorite song,
remind me each day
of how much more there is to this life.
More than just living. More than how fast we can live,
it is the time in which we can do it,
It the understanding of the value, of this life
and how many memories we leave behind,
at the end of our time here.
This is the answer to the secret of life.
Not of how many breaths we take,
but the beauty
of what takes our breath away.

Laurie, 2022

Some Day's

There are some days my heart, just needs a break.
Yet other days my mind, wants adventures.
Some days my skin, needs the touch of the sun.
Those are the days; my soul needs a breath of fresh air.
Some days my curiosity, needs different scenery.
My head needs comfort but wants stimulation.
Some days my dreams are wild, and I need a bigger space.
Some days my fears, need to be quieted.
Some days my love needs a change, my loss once safe,
I am stuck like this.
All of my days, in the hot and the cold of a human paradox
hanging somewhere,
between the sickness and the cure.
Between the sunset of yesterday
and the new dawn of tomorrow.
Unfinished like most books.
Writing new chapters of life, with every last bit of ink,
touching the pages.
Some days the shadows, of shading colors
the days and nights of life.
Nobody told me that this wild and messy of now,
could overshadow the mystery of the unknown.
That some days life could dare, to be so beautiful.
But some days, I know I will never see
all the mysteries, of secrets untold.
The bitter bite of the cold, the soft brush of the sun.
This of life.
Some days are just that
and that is
all that I know.

Laurie 2022

That is just who I am.

All of my life I have been curious
as to who I should be or who I was.
All of my life I was cautioned, about what I should wear,
or what I should look like,
how I should sound or what I should say,
even when, I should say it.
I tried to do what I was told, but it just didn't take.
I tried to stay in the background, but that just didn't work either.
I was never happy, being made to fit into the mold,
or into those small drab boxes.
So, I stopped trying to fit in.
I realize now that each person is unique, in their own way.
But I want more than what everyone else, seems to be
satisfied with.
I want to do what everyone else, is afraid of doing.
Anything else is a disaster for me, I get bored too quickly.
I can't and I won't ever do anything quietly or halfway.
I'm not afraid to put myself out there and take the risk.
To build that bridge and be the first one to try it,
sure, I've been burnt more than my fair share.
But I won't stop trying, to make this world a better place to be.
It's a risk I'm willing to take, day after day
because the reward is worth the tears and the heartache,
at any price.
I know many will never agree with me on that,
but it is my choice, and I'll take that chance again and again
without the slightest hesitation.
I spent many sleepless nights convincing
myself to try and sleep,
or tossing and turning, in restless turmoil.
Completely unable to sleep because my mind never stops.
But that's just part of it, part of who I am,

and I have come to accept that part of me.
I refuse to stop living and stop loving
because I've had my heart taken away.
I have learned from my mistakes,
and I have built higher walls
around my heart,
but I still give too much of myself away.
That's just who I am.
I live every day to the fullest,
and I love life, with my whole heart.
Because that, again, is just who I am.
I don't plan on changing that part of me, it's who I am.
Anything that I do, is all or nothing.
So, if you think you're going to come into my life
with some form of lackluster passion.
Or part time friendship.
Think again.
I'm always there for my people and I always will be,
but I expect the same, although I seldom get it.
I wear my heart on my sleeve and I speak my mind.
That's just who I am when it comes to life.
I don't need grandiose promises or fancy dreams.
I yearned for real, authentic, and genuine love,
deep feeling, soul touching, heart stimulating,
and an honest emotional connection.
Anything less isn't enough for me, never will be.
I'm sure that most will shake their heads in disapproval,
at the way I live or think.
They're welcome to pass judgment on me,
if they deem that the right way too be.
It doesn't mean I will care, listen, or even take heed.
They don't know where I've been, nor
do they know my reasons,
so, they don't have a clue who I am.
Even if they think they know me, because they don't have a clue.

I don't even know me, so.
I'm going to keep rushing hard into each and every day
with everything I have.
No matter how hard the challenge may be,
I was born to become more.
And that's just what I'm doing.
Big Heart, big hopes, big dreams, and it all starts with me.
I'll keep taking the chances for life.
Because just like I always do, that's just who I am.
I'm going to keep loving life, working with a passion
for change and living with my whole heart.
It's now or never, so I am choosing now.
That's just who I am.
And that's just what I do.

Laurie 2022

One More Time

The beat of the drum does not stop, nor will it pause.
Not even for a moment, will it slow down long
enough, to allow me to get my bearings.
Not even, to rest and try to start again.
If the Sages are right,
and it is I who creates my own destiny,
then please cut that part, out of me.
That part which hides me from a love,
that understands the depths of this soul and a heart,
that needs a meaning or a purpose.
Show me the one who has glimpsed the mystery,
who has undertaken the quest for the unanswerable.
And I'll show you the one,
who will not-cannot accept skin deep
but seeks life, to the marrow of their bones.
Do not build for yourself a prison
and put God's name on the door,
for that which you have tried to contain or restrain.
Because it will not be molded by your hands,
not by your hands alone.
That spark that gave your life, also gave life to me,
and I need not feel its breathing, to know it dwells within me.
Do not bleed in silence, for what you have sought
but not yet found,
found but not yet kept.
For the many tears you have held inside.
For the tears you have not yet wept.
Let words of life fall from your lips,
like notes escaping a precious melody.
Let it fill your days with shared happiness and laughter,
shared with the one who sees past and into the shadows
of your mind.

Those with more understanding of the
mysteries, that even you do not.
For that is the one, who will hold your heart
until the ending of your time.
When the last melody has been sung,
the last word has been recorded,
down to the last rhyme.
That keeper of your heart will hold you close
as the chaos flows through your soul
one more time.

Laurie 2022

The Melody of Me

A hidden library of long-lost memories
and melodies, within my mind.

As I sit... I hear the long fading sounds,
long lost fading memories of notes made.
As if on a piano,
each note and stroke of each key
as if it echoes and ebbs over me.
The keys that were touched, to form these long-lost melodies.
I'm sifting through my mind tonight....
I sit and listen, as some are light, almost flirty notes,
while others are deep resonating sounds,
echoing deep within my mind.
I close my eyes and try to imagine,
it's as if the hands of God
running over the piano keys.
As if he is trying to help us balance our Life's Melody.
Melodies and Piano keys are like the letters of the Bible,
singing out our memories, accomplishments,
our failures, triumphs, even our victories in life.
The white keys represent happiness
and the black keys
represent sadness.
As we go through life's journey, we have to remember
that even in sadness, the black keys can also create music.
And although the piano keys are all black and white,
they sound like a million colors resounding in your mind.
Recalling a memory, reminding us of a past loved one.
Remembering the feeling of loss.
Love is the hand that plays, touching one key or another
to cause the emotions and vibrations
echoing through our soul.

Our life is like a piano.
The melody of the memories you can get
from it, are in the keys, you choose to play.
Each and every single moment of the day.
I wonder how the memory of me, will someday be played?
The sounds that each memory will make.
As the hands, play over the keys,
expressing the emotions, I hope you will think of me,
As you let it play the melody of my life,
echoing softly,
through your memories.

Laurie 2022

Winter

The soft white snowflakes had slowly arrived.
Throughout the night, climbing higher
and higher, against my window.
I am sitting in my chair, watching them gently fall,
amazed at their quietness one upon the next,
the peaceful lull, a pause in time.
Slowly adding up, to form drifts, blowing across
the landscape of the forest.
I let my mind wander out through the
memories, to a favored location of mine.
The cliffs were never one to disappoint,
no matter the season presented.
I observed in my mind, as the snowflakes artfully lined
the branches of the varied trees, and shapes that showed
upon the craggy faces of cliffs of sandstone and bedrock.
Their purpose, now of course, was to
display the seasons change.
That was only the beginning.
For one day soon, it would be melting again,
to allow the land to absorb the moisture,
back into the land.
Their effect was mesmerizing.
This memory would serve, too last long after, the snow is gone.
The forest felt so alive, welcoming this present from above.
Such a gift, I thought, to revel in this moment.
So, I stayed a while longer, lost inside my mind,
lost in the memories of times past.
As I had leaned up to and against, the tallest of trees,
my hands pressed against a small patch of freshly fallen snow.
I love it here, this Wonderland of beauty.
I could go on for days,

as I gently tossed a handful of snow into the air.
Enjoying my time spent
among the ancient, beautiful offering,
of Winter's first snowfall.

Laurie 2022

There Are Those Day's

There are days, of which I cannot speak.
There are wishes hidden deep in my heart, that
of which can never be allowed to die.
There are thoughts, which make this strong heart weak.
Some days, to even bring a tear upon my cheek.
Sometimes a mist before the eye, in the
words of that fateful song.
Memories come over me like a dream.
A strong will, as the winds will and the
thoughts of youth, are so long gone.
Dreams of what could have been, are
now fading to the shadows
of what has been reality, is a bitter wind on these days.
But I realize the sun will always shine again.
This is but a stumble. Maybe a darker night.
Things always seem better in the light.
And night will never last forever
So, with a smile and a soft prayer, I head out for another day,
knowing I will never be truly alone.
Even though I have a moment or two here and there
that I wonder.
He is always there to catch me
and that gives me the courage
to walk this day.
Without a care.

Laurie 2022

A Moment in Time

There was a moment in time
when I would have set myself on fire
to keep another warm.
There was a moment in time
I would have crossed an ocean to reach someone
instead of swimming, to save myself.
Even someone who would not have crossed,
a shallow stream for me.
There was a moment in time
I would have tried.
And continuously tried way too hard,
just to be seen
by someone I had admired.
Who could simply never see me?
There was a moment in time
I felt myself to be unworthy of another
who would never have been worthy of me.
But not anymore.
You see, my dear, there are many ways to spend your time,
but wasting it on those, who are not worthy of your admiration
is just a crying shame.
Use your time wisely, as you will learn in your own time,
it is limited.
Save your best efforts for those, who will need it,
for those, who will appreciate that effort
or at least appreciate your attention,
those who genuinely love you,
who will never risk losing you.
And the rest?
If they do not see you now, they never will.
They will never know, what they are missing in their life
until you are gone.

Make this, the time that you realize, your time is precious too,
and should only be bestowed on those,
who bring you comfort positively.
Support, love, or joy, or all the above.
Remember, my dear, you are the main act, not a warmup.
And this life is no dress rehearsal.
This is it. It is just life.
It is what you make it and only you can make that choice.
Live and let live,
but always follow your heart and strive to be
all that you can be.

Laurie 2022

The Day's

There will be days
when all you can do is look up
because you feel you are so far down,
you can only go up from here.
Those are the days.
All you will see, are your tears falling.
Those are the days, which will be the hardest.
These days will grab the parts of your heart,
that hurt the most.
Those parts that you built, the wall around
you have kept locked up and well hidden,
for these are the parts, where you will love the most.
The parts you are most afraid, for anyone to see.
Because these are the parts that carry love,
old love, new love.
Possibly a secret love.
Those will be days when you let your crown drop,
and some days you will want to throw your crown far away.
You will experience those days,
where you will feel like it all, could be a waste of time.
You will have days where your favorite Jean's won't fit in.
Your favorite T-shirt may end up looking
like a backup piece of material or the next grease rag.
But just because some things are temporary,
does not make them any less poetic, or valuable.
That day will arrive when you realize
It is okay, to take a break.
It is okay, not to have everything perfectly together.
It is okay, to fall now and then.
It is okay, to feel anger and pain.
To fill the need to ask a question.
Even if those days, brings much needed soul searching.

These are the days, which will bring about a change.
Character will be strengthened on those days.
Those days bring healing, along with the pain.
Those days bring healing, to a broken heart.
Just accept that life happens, with all its ups and downs
and all the in-betweens.
Embrace the glorious mess that you are, even if you do it in
fashionable high heels or two differently colored socks.
You are worth every second of it.
You are worthy of Love, Respect, Happiness, and Pure Gold.
You are worthy of being a Princess, a Hero, Queen of the World.
You are a Masterpiece.
You are a Woman.
You are God's one-of-a-kind Creation.
Don't ever allow anyone,
no matter who they are
or how highly they think themselves to be,
to tell you otherwise
or to make you feel less
than the absolute miracle
that you are.

Laurie 2022

A Single Leaf

The wind blows, as if in gusts.
I notice it detaching a single leaf,
off the tree outside my window.
The tree has so many leaves,
but just one is taken with the wind.
It is, as if it is an example of a sweet soul, taken away too soon.
With so many in this world, one hardly
misses just one sweet soul
gone as the leaf, was in the wind.
Yet as with this soul,
this one single leaf you would hardly see a difference,
because one, is nearly none.
Yet that one soul alone,
was a vital part of someone's life.
That is why, as the wind continues in to blow,
I realize.
We will always miss this one single leaf alone.
For we never know that final moment when in the wind,
we lose that single soul or leaf, never to fall again.

Laurie, 2022

A Girl

There's a girl in my mirror
and she looks a lot like me
She seems to be looking back at me.
I am astonished to see this girl
But as I reach, far back into my memories,
I think of all the things, those blue eyes have seen.
Though there's lines around my eyes now,
and some gray in my hair,
That younger version of me, I remember that long hair,
was wild and free.
I'm a bit older than I remember.
I should only be twenty-three.
Did I miss the day this happened?
Have I always been this way?
And in the eyes of this woman,
whose eyes, I am seeing in the mirror,
those eyes have an air of calm.
Something of a relaxed grace, like a tide that's going out
or one of belonging on a beach that soft and warm.
These eyes have seen the world in color,
seen it in the days of grey,
and they have learned, to know the truth.
There's a wisdom in her smile now.
There's a knowledge that wasn't there
before, matured from her youth.
In her smile, she seems to move more freely,
as though released from earthly binds.
Is she made of something lighter?
Perhaps the weight of the past, that's left
behind, like the press of expectation,
with no need to yield or bend.

I smile at this woman in the mirror.
She's fast becoming
my best friend.

Laurie 2022

Set Her Free

They said that she was too wild.
They said that she is too passionate.
Her dreams had no boundaries.
No adventure was ever off limits.
Laughter was her only medicine, a wild hearted Angel.
She was never a cookie cutter type.
Her tongue is sharp, her wit is keen.
She was never meant to be tamed.
If your energy can't match hers.
Then she would be too intense for you.
She is not one, for the weak of heart,
nor for someone, who can't treat her as an equal.
She is what the old timers would call, a spirited woman.
Some may even call her difficult, always too much to handle.
But to win her heart, would be a prize to ponder,
for through life, she may wander here and there.
But if you hold her heart, she will always return.
Just give her freedom to be, who she needs to be.
In time, she will slow down.
That is needed for flexing her wings.
She will return home, but only if you first,
you learn to set her free.

Laurie 2022

This moment

As I look back over my unusual and exciting life,
replaying all the memories, of all the
amazing and unique places
I have been.
Memories of all the amazing people, I've met along the way.
Many still stand out to me as precious memories,
special markers, to mark my years.
In time, even to this day, they stand out as a special moment,
to hold in my memories, shining brightly in my mind.
As if a shaft of light came down from
heavens, marking that place,
to be perfectly preserved in time.
I could feel it all around me, within me.
Filling up the spaces in my heart, something different
about some places, something that told me to stop
and take a moment to really look and see.
And when you feel like that, at least when I felt it, I stopped.
I took some time to look around, trying to take everything in
so that I could remember it in the future of every single detail.
Just so I could remember and learn from it, to
draw from it, as I would need it in the future.
I should have remembered to give thanks to God
and enjoy what he had wanted me to see.
To learn, to feel, to understand and to experience,
what he had shown me as only he could do.
And to stop and see the wonder of it all, but I didn't
really understand any of that, until now.
It was here, walking in these forests, exploring these beaches,
on the lakes and cool, clear streams, that
I actually felt time stands still.
As the sun shines upon my face, or maybe as my fingers
brushed through the waves, just to stand and see.

For time to stand still........ if only for a moment.
I can see the sun's rays as they cut through the clouds,
the swaying leaves above so effortlessly, in the breeze.
Painting unique patterns across lower forest floor,
so completely covered with softly scented pine needles,
making a fragrant carpet to walk upon.
This was a picture only God could create.
Then for a moment listening, as a breath softly whispers
on the wind, a message oh so quiet but oh, so noticeably clear.
"I made this day, all for you",
I heard the whisper fall upon my ear.
There in that moment, in this space of time,
I see the birds flutter gently through
the trees so high above it all.
I realized why, I had wondered so far in
my life, aimlessly for so long.
It is here that I stand in awe, marveling
at the clarity of what I see.
Of what was created just for me, just for this moment in my life,
just for this moment.

Laurie 2022

Thoughts On a Mother?

Somebody said it takes about six weeks,
to get back to normal after you have had a baby.
That somebody does not know, that once you're a mother,
normal is history.
Somebody said you learn how to be a mother, by instinct.
That somebody never took a 3-year-old shopping.
Somebody said being a mother is boring.
That is somebody who has never ridden in a car,
driven by a teenager,
with a brand-new drivers permit.
Somebody said that if you are a good mother,
Your child will turn out good.
That somebody thinks a child comes with directions
and a guarantee.
They do not.
They just do not come into our lives that way.
Somebody said good mothers never raised their voices.
That is someone who has never came out the back door
just in time to see her child throw a ball,
through the neighbor's kitchen window.
Somebody said you don't need an education to be a mother.
That's somebody who has never helped a fourth grader
with "simple" math.
Somebody said you can't love the fifth child as much,
as you love the first.
That somebody doesn't have five children.
Somebody said a mother can find all the answers
to her child rearing questions, on Google or in the books.
That somebody never had a child stuff beans or Legos
up his nose or in his ears.
Somebody said the hardest part of being
a mother is labor and delivery.

That somebody never watched her baby
get on the bus, headed for the first day of kindergarten
or on a plane, headed for boot camp.
Somebody said a mother can do her job with her eyes closed
and one hand tied behind her back.
That somebody never tried to organize squiggly little toddlers
and keep them focused and quiet.
Somebody said a mother can stop worrying
after a child gets married.
That somebody doesn't know
that that marriage adds a new son or a daughter-in-law
to tug on a mother's heartstrings.
Somebody said a mother's job is
done, when her last child leaves Home,
that somebody never had grandchildren.
Somebody said your mother knows you love her,
so, you don't need to tell her
Well, all that I can say is
That somebody isn't a mother.

Laurie 2022

Time

If time has taught me anything, it is
that the tiny spot in this universe that I inhabit,
is both wonderful and chaotic.
And if I allow it too just be,
then the world around me can unlock the beauty, within me
and teach me the beauty in this life.
Life has shown me, far more than any schooling ever could
if time, has taught me anything.
It should be that success and how we measure time,
needs to be refined.
And the only person to whom I should ever compare myself to,
Is myself and who I was yesterday.
Time has made my growth game strong.
Time has taught me, that somewhere along the way
I will learn to take time to be kind to myself,
but only if I am doing my best.
Well then, I need to learn that I am doing enough,
If time has taught me anything.
It would be more important now, than ever before
to see the world through my own eyes,
and not through someone else's point of view.
Beginning to break that habit only by
looking at myself honestly,
looking and gently judging,
looking inward at my own self, with wisdom and kindness.
Also looking outward, with compassion and appreciation.
If time has taught me anything, it should be that the opposite
of love is not hate, but fear, and my greatest fear is losing
those to which I have become so attached.
Yesterday was heavy, I need to learn to put
it down and leave it where it belongs.
To see the beauty around me in all this world, where I reside.

That should be the first step in life to clear
all the shadows in my mind
of all the past, putting them down to be
used only as steppingstones,
building the present to be so much stronger.
And if time has taught me anything,
It is that nature, unlike us, never apologizes for her beauty.
If time has taught me anything,
It is that life, really, really Is all about
the journey, the destination,
as it must be.
For surely, we are not here merely, to reach the end,
for the destination is death, and that is not the end.
Time has taught me to be alive.
For after all this, life is all that you can make it to be.
So, when you pay attention to the things,
for which you are grateful
for then you soon forget all about, what
you thought you were missing.
If time has taught me anything,
It is that bitter tears are the quietest,
and no sound can be heard, from a broken heart.
And on the days when your head wants to hang low,
It is important that you look up.
Lift your head and enjoy the sunshine.
Take it all in and breathe in deep.
For while this world can sometimes be a hard place,
your reality and what you perceive it to be, are seldom aligned.
If time has taught me anything,
It is that beauty truly is, in the eye of the beholder.
We can see a complete world, within another world.
And only when we truly pay enough attention, that is,
when this new life, will truly become a life.
It is as true as the heart that beats within us.
As the nature around us.

If this time has taught me anything, it is this.
Some say true love conquers all.
That love will give me the strength and the fortitude, to do so.
Knowing that I am more, than my scars, knowing that every
wound in my heart, that may have been healed along the way.
Time has taught me, what life truly is.
To want to fight back, for what I believe in and start again,
from where I am, with what I have, what
I have learned and conquered.
As my fears of the unknown, cutting my own pathway
without seeking the approval of others,
and knowing that loving of who I am
is not a bad thing anymore.
If time has taught me anything,
It is this.
Hope matters, and we cannot live without it.
Time has taught me, that faith is not a wish,
nor a desire for things to be different.
It is a course of action, a combination of mind and heart,
a faith of promise for better things, the courage to believe
for things yet unseen or unknown.
The future can be better and can be brighter,
and we each have the power within our hearts to make it so.
There will still be challenging days along the way,
for which there will be many prayers and many solutions,
there is a source of resilience, a deep
desire to survive within us all.
If this time does not teach us, that time itself is precious,
then we will have missed the joy, of the lesson.
The lesson, that never before in the past,
or the future, been so irrelevant.
And that the quest to find we have been fruitless till now.
To find that answer only because we
have been searching for so long,
in all the wrong places.

We are here.

We are now.

We are each and every breath we take, every tear we shed each time our heart breaks.

We are here.

Every day is a gift, a gift to begin again.

And to grasp with both hands the fresh opportunity to learn.

To unlearn and relearn our mistakes.

To learn that this time and to realize that time is not wasted.

We will have spent it wisely

When we begin to live again.

If time has taught me anything,

Laurie, 2022

To my Grandkids

Never forget how much I love you
as you grow older, as you face the many challenges in life.
Just do your best.
It will always enough.
Life isn't about waiting, for the storm to pass
or waiting for the clouds to clear.
It's all about learning how to dance in the rain,
to stand and enjoy the wind,
just watching the storm clouds roll past, as the sky clears.
And to be thankful for each breath you take,
as you begin to see the sun, break on the horizon.
Every day may not be perfect,
but find something good, in every day.
Laugh, live, find the best, of every moment you have.
Follow your dreams and believe in yourself, as I believe in you.
Remember,
Grandma thinks you're awesome and totally unbeatable.
I'll always be with you.
No matter how far you may go,
as long as the sun shines or the moons glow touches you
as it lights in the morning or in the night sky,
I'm just a heartbeat away.
You're always in my thoughts and my prayers.
My heart is with you, no matter how far apart we may seem.
Keep this tucked away in your heart and in your memories.
You may have a rough day and think all is lost.
That's when I hope, you think of me.
Because no matter the day,
no matter the time,
you will always,
always be on my mind.

Love Grandma

Laurie 2022

Your Gift

There is always plenty to be upset about,
but almost all of these things are outside of my control.
Those things that are in my control,
are the things I can be thankful for.
And I can spend all day expressing,
my gratitude for those.
If you really wanted me to start,
the list would be almost infinitely endless.
It's not that I choose to ignore the reality of things.
They can still cause frustration and stress,
but neither should I allow those things to
consume all of my attention.
Or to the point, where I think that everything
is over and no use even trying anymore.
This gift of life is greater than all these frustrations.
The gift of life is just that.
A gift.
And it's mine right now.
It's yours.
The air we breathe, a gift
The body we are breathing that air into.
This world, that we live within is, a gift.
The sun, the moon, the trees, the breeze,
the love, the stars, the hills, the shade, the water,
all of these are gifts.
All we can see here smell, touch, taste, all are gifts.
The people in our life, are gifts,
Our parents, children, friends, partner, all of them, all are a gift.
Your ideas, your talents, your courage, your blessings,
They are all a gift.
We did not purchase our life; it was given to us.

There are bad things going on in this world,
but it's not the only thing going on.
Don't lose yourself in the bad news.
Remember the good things
and who you are, who God is.
There is still an abundance to be thankful for
and to be excited about,
but only when you give it the attention it deserves.
That's when we see all, that we are
blessed with and who we are.
Just breathe.
Stop listening to whatever station to which you are listening.
Turn off the noise of the day and just breathe.
Tune out technology.
Tune into nature.
Tune into yourself.
Tune into the reason for life.
Listen closely, It's good news.
This is your gift.

Laurie 2022

What If?

What if we try to see the good in people
more than looking to the bad
or trying to find everything they are doing wrong?
What if we try harder to see the positive
of what we're trying to do,
instead of seeing only the negative
that seems to bring out the worst in ourselves and others.
What if we gave others, the benefit of the doubt?
More than doubting their motives or
questioning their intentions.
What if we looked at the ways, they were always there,
to love you through the good and the bad, showing up for you,
being there when needed?
Never asking for anything in return.
More to those times, rather than the few times
they may not have known we needed help or didn't show up.
What if?
What if we genuinely believed that we all have those bad days?
Those days when we stumble and fall?
Days when we feel alone without a friend in the world.
Those days we cannot understand why.
What if we agree to disagree,
realizing that we do not know everyone's stories,
we do not know their pain, we don't know their past,
their fears, their memories that come back to haunt them
when at their lowest point?
What if we all realize most times, we really do not know?
Are those reasons,
the reasons behind the things they do or say?
Maybe that is the way it is, and but it will still be okay.
What if we extended grace more freely,
as we would want it extended, towards us?

What if we let go of resentment
and leaned into forgiveness more?
What if we just take a deep breath and let it go,
more than we usually do?
What would that do?
What if we had more deliberation in our days?
Taking the time to have real and honest conversations,
when we are hurt,
rather than fall into quiet, passive aggressiveness
and assume they should just know, how we feel?
What if we just keep trying to pry our
broken and scarred hearts
open a little more?
So, we could let someone in and allow
the fear and distrust out more.
What if we accepted the fact, that we don't always believe
in the same things as or want the same things,
but could we still coexist together, even thrive together?
What if we just decided today to honestly
believe, that we are all trying our best?
What if we all kept giving our hearts, over to good?
Let God do a work in them, so we can be better friends,
parents, partners and neighbors, sisters, or brothers.
So, we can be a better example, of who he is
to those who have no idea or don't even know him.
What if?
I'm willing to keep trying, even when it's so hard,
and I have made every argument, as to why I shouldn't.
I will stumble and I will fall short of every one of these things,
But I'm going to keep trying and then trying some more.
Each and every day I walk in this life.
What if we greet each new day, with a renewed encouragement
and more grace and patience?
What if we go heavy on the grace and lighter on the negativity?

I'm saying that more for me
because the Lord knows, I can sure flip flop those two.
What if we just enjoy the sunrise,
and decide to enjoy the gift
we have been given.
Each and every new day?
What if?

Laurie's 2022

Free To Be Me

When he told me, I was never going to be enough,
I was broken apart.
But looking back now, I can't help but smile.
Now I know that to be anything, but the truth.
I was more than he could fathom or understand,
too much for him to manage or control.
He was letting me go
not because I wasn't enough, but because he wasn't enough.
Where once he had been attracted to
my fire and passion for life.
He soon realized
I was a person too intent on growth and progress.
He now feared that growth,
My ambitions and dreams, my passion for life.
He feared my fire would consume him.
It was then, I understood completely that he would never
have been able to keep up with the change, not in my world.
And he could never have been content,
just being in the shadows.
It was in this moment that I realized, that while many say
they embraced change, standing in front of the unknown
takes more courage, than he could find within himself.
A courage he didn't have but hated to admit.
And it was easier to place that fault upon me.
To have the courage to step out, to be terrified of your dreams
and yet, push thru anyway.
To become more, than you ever have dreamed possible,
that was what he could never do.
He just didn't understand that unfathomable part of me.
No safety nets or backup plans.
Just life, as full and fast as we could make it fly by.

But some, as he did, have to stay in their
comfortable little circle of their life.
No change, no daydreams of life or what if's.
And there is nothing wrong with that at all, but that kind of life,
just that it was not for me.
I have learned that that is not my idea of living.
He was not my kind of person.
He lacked the dream, the vision to see what I saw.
He was afraid to dream out of context.
He was terrified of my dreams.
That meant change and that, just could not be.
I now realized he was not hurting my heart, by his words.
He was setting me free, to live my dreams.
To follow my thread of pure imagination,
with only the sky as the limit.
I will always be too much of all the right
things, for the wrong people.
I realized that now, after so many false starts and dead ends.
That's why I'm going to go, where my dreams are, where
the people that don't just sit and play it safe are.
They see the stars as I do.
There will always be moments in your life when
you realize greater truths, and this was one of
my own truths, a simple one in fact.
Instead of constantly apologizing for my fierce passion,
my dreams and my intense wanderlust.
I have decided to embrace my dreams and listen to my heart,
my mind racing, with the thoughts and the possibilities.
I'll never have to chase the love, of the right people.
The ones that actually get me, who want to keep
pace with me, and they will understand.
They will welcome me with a smile and let me roam,
knowing I cannot be contained or controlled.
I am a force of my own.

Because I will never be that person who everyone understands,
and I would never seek to be.
I understand that now.
And truthfully, it is okay that is how I like it.
Wild dreams, loving life, living one hundred
miles an hour and my mind running free.
Maybe to people like him
I sound fun until they realize that they
cannot take my dreams away
or fit me into a box.
But to me, those qualities are everything.
Those are the things that make me, as I am.
Who I will always be.
And I am not changing for anything,
or anyone as I did before.
I have finally found me
and I have decided that I like me.
Just the way that I am, and the right people will.
If given the chance too.
If they set me free to dream.

Laurie, 2022

As God Intended

When she was sitting at the back of the room,
They said she was distant and cold
not realizing she was just shy
as she tried her best just to hide.
When she led from the front, as they pushed her to,
they hated her, said she has too much pride,
she was just seeking the attention.
They asked her advice, barely letting her finish,
before questioning her guidance.
Never trusting, in the wisdom of her words,
they branded her pushy and loud.
When she finally spoke up for herself,
then they were shocked.
Then struck by her silence,
when she stepped back and walked away
leaving them alone, in the mess they had made.
She would never make it in the real world,
she hadn't a clue of reality, they said.
They told her
you had better stay closer to home, you will
never make in the world alone.
When she shared no ambition, they said it was sad,
She didn't have a clue, what life was about.
So, then she told them her dreams,
the places she wanted to see and where she wanted to go,
they said she was mad.
She would never make it alone.
All those crazy ideas and far away dreams,
she would never accomplish anything that way,
They told her they would listen, to her thoughts and aspirations,
then covered their ears because she was just a dreamer.
She would never get anywhere.

They gave her a hug, feeling sympathy for her simpleness,
while they laughed at her fears,
telling her to go home, she would be safer there.
And as she listened to all of this, thinking she should.
Maybe she should listen to all of the
advice, that they have given.
Maybe it was good thing
to be the simple girl,
they told her to be.
She tried to do the best as she could,
although it was killing her inside.
But one day she stopped,
and she asked what was best for herself.
What did she want?
Instead of trying to please everyone else,
who did she want to be?
And as she thought back, to what she
had been told time after time.
How she felt, when her dreams lay fallow,
and her hope was all but lost.
She thought back to all the times she had allowed herself to
be pushed back, because she felt she was never enough.
She was either too little or far, far too much,
too loud or too quiet, too fierce, or too
weak, too wise, or too foolish,
too bold or sometimes even too meek.
But she was exactly everything, God had created her to be.
She was enough, but not too much.
She was proud and independent, but not more
than he had intended for her too be.
She was quiet yet; he had made her fiercely loyal
to those she loved.
She was wise, but not boastful or foolish as some may think.
Just confident in her way of thoughts and
confident in her ways of speech.

She was strong in her own way, never too weak.
These were the answers, to all the questions she did seek.
She was enough.
She was what everyone, said she couldn't be.
And in that moment, she realized she
had been that girl all along.
They were just too afraid, to let her see,
that she could be everything,
they would never have been brave enough to be.
She had flown higher, than any had seen, for
she was no longer afraid of her wings.
In life, she was so much more than any of her dreams
could have been before.
For she was enough.
This is what they were afraid she might be.
If she ever found out, who she could really be.
And the world opened before her.
She could see that, only the sky's was the limit.
And she even challenged that, on some day's
as if to say I am enough,
but I will be more with each and every day.
I am a dreamer.
Life knows no bounds
because I am enough.
Just As Exactly
As God Had Intended, Me to Be.

Laurie 2022

When You Look Back

I pray that you never see
the memories of your life, in ashes.
Hope you never let your fear, become your prison.
Never let your flaws become your cage and your imperfections
of your wondrous soul, build a wall
in a tower of self-doubt and fear of an unknown.
When you look back,
may you never regret the lakes you didn't swim in,
the beaches, you didn't leave your cares upon,
or the moments, you hid away from the world.
All because your image, did not meet someone's expectations.
When you look back, I pray that you vividly recall the moments
of joy, as the moonlight shone in the path.
Or when the sun came out and the world
opened, like a flower to sunlight.
Or to let you wander through a forest through its very heart and
soul.
Or to stand under a vivid sunset,
to see it mirrored upon the surface of lake.
When you look back, may you see that
you were always enough.
Contentment was always the goal; peace
was its chariot and hope abounded.
Love was the gentle breeze, to help speed it along.
I hope you shared that wisdom, you learned along the way,
with others, who may have so desperately needed it.
When you look back,
may you know that your life was one well lived.
That the occasional heart breaks, you had no control over.
They were only storms in your blue skies.
And not an unrequited love, for your own self
that darkened your entire journey.

When you look back,
may you breathe easy,
safe in the knowledge you blazed a path.
That you have made a special difference in someone's life,
whilst on this journey.
Spreading joy, spreading light, breaking, and rebuilding,
always giving, of your beautiful heart freely.
For that is all you're really here to do,
making your time here in life.
The best version of you.

Laurie 2022

What It Is

When you see her,
You may see a warm smile and a gentle, caring nature.
Most will never understand her
Most will never have the courage to see past, her tough facade
that protects who she truly is.
You will never know her journey through the fire
and the battle to reshape herself,
While still twisting within the flames of her past.
And she is okay, with that.
She will never be that person, who shares her thoughts freely.
The ones who truly get her,
are the ones that have taken the time,
to look past the curtain covering her eyes.
Her circle is the loved ones, who accept her
for all of her flaws, scars, and scratches.
Those who love and accept her, for who she is
not for what she can do for them or what she can give,
but because she is a marvelous creature.
Once you fully begin to fully grasp,
the layers of her depth, who she has become.
You will wonder how you could ever miss seeing her
as to who she really is.
She will always be fierce in her loyalty and flawless in her love.
She's the one there in the midst of the chaos,
when people need someone the most.
She will be there to help,
without regard to herself or what it will cost.
She's rebuilt herself over and over
each and every time she was knocked down.
Countless times,
she will never forget the failures
that pushed her to find a way, through the fire.

You will learn that her past, will never define her
Nor will her future be limited, by what she has been told,
she can and can't do.
She's been broken in the most beautiful ways
so that the light,
will always get in to illuminate her soul.
The cracks, filled with soft gold
as in the customs of old
if they are broken or damaged.
She doesn't hide her scars,
but remembers each bruise, quietly and privately.
Because those are the lessons life has taught her.
It has taught her, how to discover herself, her
strengths and to control her weaknesses.
Yet no one else needs to ever know.
So, if you want to try to understand,
the true nature of a woman like her.
prepare yourself for a lifetime to learn her nature.
So be patient and earn her trust,
to see into her depths and explore the hidden beauty
that lies within.
She is fragile, like a firestorm,
struggling to stay standing, in the winds of a hurricane.
Strong like a wildflower, yet soft as a
newborn baby, on some days.
Never predictable and but always passionate
in every facet of her life.
She will love you like a wildfire
then leave you twisting and turning within the flames,
sometimes needing the rain to quench the burn
but always going back for more.
Shall never be just a woman.
She's unique and she thinks as few do.
She is expecting to be misunderstood,
As she knows she is not going to be the same

as anyone else.

And then......... you will only scratch the surface,

of who she is,

yet even then you'll never begin to understand.

That there's so much more to her, than meets the eye.

You could have known her for years,

but still will never know her deep inside.

You will never forget meeting her,

she will be in your memories, for years to come,

as only she can.

With a warrior's heart and a poetic soul,

She's more than just one-of-a-kind,

she is a once in a lifetime woman.

You'll always remember the moment when you

met her, and the moment she was gone.

And this time will have changed your life,

if only it too, but for a second in time.

You will never forget that smile and the amazing strengths,

as she holds her thoughts quiet within.

Until she speaks to you with a quiet deliberation,

of all her thoughts and whims.

You see the bravery of this woman, proud and strong,

as you look into her eyes,

you may even feel yourself drawn into their depths.

But she is not one that will lead you on,

not with her blunt honesty and manner of speaking.

She is who and what she says she is.

Make no mistake and take her at her word,

for she will stand strong for what she believes.

But do not expect her to change, for that she cannot do.

She is exactly what you see, and that will always be her.

So, if changing her is what you hold in your mind,

please do not waste your time or hers, for that will not happen.

Not in this lifetime.

She has spent years building her life back,

one brick at a time, and she guards so carefully
who enters that life now.
If you come into her life without true intentions,
she can burn you to the ground, with just her eyes.
She will forgive you, but she will never
forget or trust you that far again.
Her silence will be unbroken, for you in the future.
But if you come as a true friend,
one she can count on through thick and thin,
she will give you a love in return, along with her kindness.
Yet if you seek to change her, she will also walk away,
with a polite smile and leave you behind her.
No malice or ill intent, will she hold against you,
but her life, is her life.
And she needs that will to survive.
Take her at her word, for she will stand.
For what she sees.
Her motto in life.
Is
"It is, what it is"
And that is what, it will be.

Laurie 2022

Words

They say the things that finally break you will
be the words, which were left unspoken.
With years and years of words unspoken,
pushed into the emptiness of time.
With so many thoughts not uttered,
crammed into all the corners,
in the back of your mind.
A careless whisper, lost in a world of noise.
Where this world knows only how to listen,
not with the intent to hear, but only with the intent to speak.
Where the silence, they say must be broken
to prove that you are not weak.
But where she wonders, lies the weakness holding the words,
inside your own mind.
When others listen to reply, she listens to understand,
showing her strength, with words unspoken.
Filling the empty spaces of the room,
When other's flounder, in the multitudes of spoken words,
She is the one that knows how to swim.
For in this world of utter chaos,
she is the calm, in the eye of the storm,
waiting in the quiet, to understand why.
Why?
Too few seek the answers, to the unspoken questions,
as she has flowing through her mind.
But as the wind dies down, she hears those answers,
as if on the last breath of the wind.
As she softly smiles, taking her time to walk quietly,
through the shadows of the night.
She has found her answers upon the lakeshores, again.

Laurie, 2022

Meant To Be

You are strong enough to survive this, although
I know that it feels like your dreams
crushed and your life is over.
They may never come true, as you had hoped.
Maybe you can't find the light in the dark,
right now but hang in there.
You will make it through.
I know your heart is weary and you
feel like you can't stay strong,
but don't give up the fight.
That would just be wrong.
Your happiness may seem so far away, but
it's not as far away, as it seems.
Yes, the nights are long, you don't have any answers,
but you don't have to always know the ending first.
Just slow down and learn to breathe.
Take a deep breath and repeat.
Take a moment and remember how far you have come,
how much you have overcome, against all odds,
when they never believed in you.
You have even come through the fire; you
have always found your way through.
Your courage has been forged, in the same
flames, that had burned to take you down.
Remember that you are a fighter.
Who will continue to rise again and again.
It's time to find your voice and listen to your heart.
It knows the way, even when you've gotten so weary
that you may have lost the path.
When the stars are hidden from the view, or the
moon may slide behind the clouds, the rolling
mists may even hide your way home.

Even when you've lost faith in yourself
and your strength is waning,
know that you're not alone.
You are loved.
You are always enough, always will be, and I believe in you.
The darkest hour, is always before the dawn,
and that is your time to start again, to be reborn.
Every end is a new beginning,
and your next chapter, will be so much more.
You just have to start believing in yourself, like the hero we see
when we look at you.
So, as you sit, wondering how you will
make it, through all of this,
I'm telling you; you've got this.
You are meant for more than to simply
live, like a flicker of light.
You are a Wildfire capable of setting your own soul,
and all in your life on fire, igniting the world around you.
So, as you start climbing out of the darkness, day by day,
always looking for a sign, something to believe in.
Well, this is it.
Today is your wakeup call, and this is where you start again.
You're strong enough and you're worth it all.
It won't be easy, and it won't be fast, but it
will change your life if you're ready.
These words were meant for you.
Are you ready to start again?
Believe me, darling, believe in yourself,
in your destiny, and most of all,
that you are meant for so much more.
Spread those wings.
Let the wind carry you far and away.
Beginning today, step up.
Start living, remembering all the magic and
dreams, you may have lost along the way.

As a caterpillar from the cocoon, you will emerge
with the beauty and grace, a new creation.
Forged from the fires, meant to consume you,
but instead, they forged your way to where
you were meant to be.

Laurie 2022

Enjoy The Climb

Yes. I know you're tired.
Not just a sleepy tired, but a bone deep exhaustion.
That just keeps creeping in more and more, each and every day.
As it pulls you deeper and deeper,
into that void within yourself.
You are literally on autopilot.
So, to the people on the outside,
All they see is calm and collected.
Someone who is always in charge and knows the course.
But if you were to speak the truth,
if the truth is to be told,
you are falling apart inside.
You hold it together, just long enough to get home.
So, you can fall apart behind closed doors.
But whether you realize it or not,
you are strong enough to survive this.
To not only survive, but to rise
so far above the chaos
and heartache that you feel now.
I know it seems like your world is over
and maybe you can't find the light right now
but hang in there.
It's all coming to you, all in good time.
You're still climbing that mountain,
but one day you will look up
just as you crest the peak.
You will look back down that mountain,
astonished at how you made it so far.
I know your soul is weary and you feel
like you can't keep going,
but please don't stop.
Your happiness may seem so far away,

but it's not as far as you might think.
Yes, the nights can be long, and you won't have any answers,
but you don't have to.
You're allowed to not have all the answers.
Just Breathe
Just take a deep breath in and out as a soft rhythm.
Just breathe and continue onwards.
Take a moment, if you need it,
just don't stop your forward motion.
Just try and remember, what all that you've survived before.
This is nothing compared, to the last 20 years
just a bump in the road.
You've been through the fire and always found your way.
Your courage has been found, in those hard times.
You rose from the waves as they crested and crashed
along the shore.
Yet here you are.
Remember, you're as a Phoenix
who will continue to rise again and again,
till you finally get it right.
Through it all, you will find your wings and then.
You will take flight.
Trust me.
It's time to find your magic again.
And
Listen to your heart.
Leave the memories in the past where they belong.
Look ahead at all that you have to see along that horizon.
Stand tall and watch
as the new sun rises and covers the road ahead.
It's been a long night, I agree.
But the nights never last forever.
And even then, we have the moon to see by.
Sometimes we just forget that part.
But always follow your heart.

It still knows the way.
Even when you've gotten so weary, that you've lost the path.
Even if you've lost faith in yourself and your strength is waning,
know that you are not alone.
You are loved and you are enough.
So many people believe in you.
It's always darkest before the dawn, but the sun will always rise.
This is your time to start again.
Each and every day, is a new beginning,
and your next chapter in this life,
will be worth the hardships.
You just have to start seeing you,
as you are and what others see in you,
like I do.
I know you're reading this and wondering,
how you'll make it through
the next day, week, month,
or maybe year.
I'm telling you; you've got this.
You are meant for more than to simply exist
and fizzle out
like water to a flame.
As the raindrops start to fall, you are your own wildfire,
capable of setting yourself an all-around you ablaze again.
You may not see this now,
but when you start climbing out of that valley,
slowly taking the incline day by day,
someday you will look back off the top of that mountain
and see all around you.
I know if you've been looking for a sign,
something to believe in,
well, I cannot give you that.
But then again, I really wouldn't have to.
You already know the way.
It won't be easy.

Fact is, it won't even be fast, but it will change your life.
If you're ready.
Anything's possible if you just believe and start climbing.
That rearview mirror is just that,
something to use as a reference, not to guide you.
You cannot climb that mountain looking back
behind you every day.
That's why the windshield is much larger.
That's your future.
That's where you're headed.
The sky is the limit.
Enjoy the climb

Laurie 2022

Where You Need to Be

You know those days when you wake up
and the whole world seems to be coming down,
on your shoulders?
Simply close your eyes, take a deep breath, and try again.
The best thing is,
that you do not have to have it all figured out
or even know where this day,
will take you.
There is always going to be those days,
in which you cannot seem to get anything right,
and everything just seems to fall apart.
Every time you look up, something else
is heading straight at you.
But you do not have to conquer it all in one day,
or even in that same week.
You have to stop focusing,
on the whole weight of the world
and take one step, one day at a time.
Baby steps if you have to.
One problem, one solution.
Keep trying it until you get it right.
Every one of us is a mess sometimes.
We all have moments
where we just want to cry,
give it up and walk away.
And if you need to,
just let it go and come back to fight another day.
Tackle each day, job, or task, one at a time,
and keep moving forward.
You only fail if you allow yourself to quit.
Some days you'll feel as though.
You can do nothing.

And other days you'll put your keys in the refrigerator,
or be talking to your phone,
while you're looking for it.
That's just life.
Some good days, some bad days,
and the days,
that make you want to quit.
Sometimes will outweigh the good.
You will never be perfect.
But the great thing is you don't have to be.
Do not let anyone put unrealistic expectations, on you.
they could not even do that themselves.
And never let the worry of how,
you will get all this done stress you out.
More importantly,
stop being in a hurry all the time
to do all the things and get everywhere super-fast.
You will miss some of life's greatest little moments,
if you are zooming through trying to conquer life,
without stopping to look around you.
Never get too busy Doing,
In the process, we are forgetting how to live
along the way.
Do the things. Get the job done.
You will be present.
But more than that, notice the small things,
the smell of the fresh morning dew,
all the beauty of the world around you.
The laughter of small children playing
the sound of the wind in the trees,
that is the stuff that memories are made of.
But you will miss those
if you're in a constant state of worry,
about all the things you still need to do.
Take the time to fill your heart and soul,

with the joy of your family and friends.
Don't sweat the small stuff, make them into memories.
So yes, you're going to be a mess some days,
and sometimes you'll be figuring it all out, as you go.
Just keep moving forward, step by step, and do what you can,
how you can when you can.
Most of all, don't stop living and enjoying your life.
After all, what good is it to conquer the world,
if you don't take time to enjoy it along the way,
or have someone to share it with?
Each day is a new opportunity, to start a new chapter.
Keep going.
You'll get it where you need to be,
when you need to be there.
It just takes a little time, a little effort, and a lot of patience.
Somedays you've got this one step at a time,
until one day you're exactly
where you always wanted to be.

Laurie 2022

More

You learned the hardest lesson possible,
at the worst time in your life, enduring
an unimaginable heartache.
You tried so hard to hide.
You discovered your strength at the
most difficult time, in your life.
Maybe you thought life had finally broken you,
That your heart was irreparably cracked, for all the world to see.
As you sank to your lowest point, at your very weakest in life,
you looked deep within yourself; in
places you never knew you had
or that had ever existed.
Uncovering a courageous strength, you
never knew you possessed.
When you thought you were breaking into countless pieces
of shattered chaos, you learned the most valuable truth of all.
You just let go.
What didn't make you stronger?
You let go.
Of all that keep you from growing?
Of what kept cutting so deep?
The wounds that healed, have made you the strong one,
you had come to be.
No more living for the possibilities, you were
finished trying to wait for life, waiting for the
right moment to get what you wanted.
You realize that if it were meant to be, it would be because of
you and your choices and how far you would be willing to go.
You would determine, how much you could be.
To see how far, you could push yourself to go?
Your heart, your strength, and your courage.

You battled, scraped, and clawed your way out, from beneath
rock bottom until you begin to do more than just survive.
You began to thrive.
You rose higher than you had ever believed possible,
unfurling the wings that had for so long lay
dormant you didn't even know you could fly.
Still mustering every dream that you had and unfurling those
beautiful wings, with amazement, as you flew at long last.
You were more than a survivor.
More than a warrior, you were unbreakable,
determined to rise from the ashes.
Long buried memories.
Fighting to become more and more, finding
your courage and strength,
you use this strength to fly free with
pure passion for your journey.
As sheer light burst forth from your heart,
that was once so completely broken.
It was no longer shattered, for all to see,
as the courage to keep going
swells within your soul.
You stopped doubting and started believing in yourself.
You learned in that moment, that you
weren't going to just reach the stars.
You would soar past the horizon, to pass
into the beautiful heights.
It wasn't ever going to be enough for you to
simply be beautiful, or just be enough.
You need the depth, passion, strength,
and fire in your heart and soul,
for you are more than an ordinary person,
more than anyone can see.
You hold the brightest light, in a twilight sky
and now it is your time, to shine.

Lighting this world around you and beyond for others to follow.
When they need a place to rest
from a troubled mind.

Laurie 2022

Life Will Make Sense, Again

As you sit and think through all the years of change.
It's like looking at the trunk of a tree, with each
year marked by a new ring, each in which you
can read the growth, through its years.
You see the stumbles, and each time you fell
as if you were reading the lines from a book, you know so well.
Some are marked by joy; in others you see the pain.
You can feel the emotions, showing in
each ring of growth you see.
You can actually feel the sadness and feel the
way the tears, fell like summer rains.
But in each season, you learned, and each time you grew.
Until finally, you were strong enough, to understand why.
And then you knew, that with each and every step you took,
your life changed and evolved, into what you are today.
Some changes were good.
Other steps you took along the way you used as a map
on what not to do, which road not to take.
As each and every day that passes, you're growing into
your strengths, learning how to adapt and grow.
With this new life, you are finding the
new strengths you never knew
you had new ways to see the world,
and a way to new adventures.
The wonder and the dawn, of each day.
The peace of knowing a difference,
within this life you have made.
As you change and make this new life, your heart will heal.
You will love life again if you will have the
courage to stand and remember why.
You will have learned the reason, for
the choices you have made.

You will once again be whole, moving forward to a new day.
As you sit and think,
Life begins to make sense again.

Laurie 2022

She Will Be the One

You will always know, who the stronger woman will be.
She will be the one
building another woman up, instead of tearing her down.
She will be the one fixing the other woman's crown,
without telling the whole world, that it
was crooked to begin with.
She will be the one
who will put an arm around your shoulders and help you stand.
Who wipes your tears, when you're close to giving in,
while she herself is crying or falling apart inside.
She will be the one
who will push you to reach new heights,
help you achieve those dreams, you quietly shared with her.
Because somewhere in life, she had someone who pushed her
and lent that guiding hand.
She will be the woman
who will make you feel like you are enough,
because she knows how it feels to feel inadequate.
She will be the one
when you feel that you are not able to go another day,
that will push you, just one more time.
Because she knows that no matter what,
when you have a positive attitude and faith,
miracles can and will happen.
She will be the one
who has a hopeful smile on her face in the morning,
when she cried herself to sleep the night before.
Pouring her heart out, while laying her burdens down
and just trying to stay whole.
She will be the one
who will silently carry you in prayer when she's so desperately
needing it herself.

She will be the one
who will defend you when you have become the target.
When she knows you're not around, to defend yourself.
She will be the woman that will helps you
when you are fighting to survive just one more day.
Not because she has that much,
but because she knows, how hopeless it feels
to have nothing at all.
She will be the woman
that the world needs more of
in the days to come.

Laurie, 2022

As You Live

Your smile is a present to the world.
You are a unique creation.
You are one-of-a-kind.
Your life can be anything you want it to be.
Live the days, just one day at a time.
Live to the fullest and in all the joy, that you can find.
Count your blessings, but not your troubles.
Those you will leave behind.
You will always make it through,
no matter what you do.
It doesn't matter, what may come along.
Within you are so many answers, yet to be known.
You hold untold inner strength, please understand this.
Have courage, be strong.
If you're still trying, you will never be wrong.
You're never a quitter unless you give up.
Never allow anyone to put limits on you.
Some waiting rooms, are just waiting to be lived in,
to be discovered.
Dedication will be important, but always
be willing, to take that chance.
Even though you're unsure, reach for that
mountain peak, your goal, and your prize.
You can never, ever reach too high.
Nothing wastes more energy, than worry and stress.
The longer one carries a grudge, the heavier it gets.
Never take yourself too seriously.
Live a life of possibilities, not a life of regrets.
Remember that a little love, goes a long way.
Bitterness is like a flat tire, you will never
go anywhere, until you change it.
Remember that a little faith in yourself, goes on forever.

Remember that friendship is a wise choice, if it's meant to be,
if it's the right one, even if it's the wrong
one, it's still just a lesson.
Life's treasures, you ask?
Are all of our memories together?
The memories we leave behind will memorialize
us forever, whether good or bad.
Realize that it is never too late, to make a new start.
Do ordinary things, in an extraordinary way,
having a heart that believes in hope and
searches for happiness, along the way.
Take the time to wish upon a star and don't ever forget,
not even for a day, how incredibly special you really are.
And how many lives, you have already
touched and will continue to touch.
What a difference your life, will make
in the life of someone else.
For that is the life, along with a treasure
of memories, you alone,
can give to those of the loved ones and friends.
A legacy you will someday, leave behind.
For this you may only need, but a day, in this life you make.
But make that day last forever,
as you live.

Laurie 2022

Upon A Lilies Bloom

Just beyond the horizon,
beneath the sky of smokey reds, yellows, and tangerines.
Is the shadow of a woman kneeling, with her head bowed low.
Her silhouette makes such a paintable scene.
As she calls up towards the heavens,
with a heart that's frail and torn, broken, and confused.
She wishes now, she'd never been born!
Humbly, she begins to tell the Lord,
she can no longer, find the hope to carry on.
As she calls upon Him, to take her now,
before the early shadows of dawn.
She blames herself, for the loss she has borne this night,
that of her child.
On what was supposed to be the start,
of his precious little life.
Of a child she would never know.
She would never hold or watch him grow.
One who perished in the dark hours of the dawn.
Memories of a child.
That would never take a breath.
Surely,
God hear my prayers, she pleads.
As she struggles with the guilt, of how she is still
alive, the heartbreaking pain of her loss.
The dawn is still and silent,
as if it's quietly listening,
as she tells the Lord her anguish, all that's in her heart.
Without her child, she doesn't think she can survive.
She hugs his blankets to her chest with sorrow,
as she screams his name, up to the heavens.
Lord, please give me an answer.
I need to know why, at least the reason why.

My dream was only, for him to live his
life, to be loved and to grow.
Why couldn't you take mine instead?
Why would you have taken my baby, instead of taking me?
Can you give me an answer, I just need to know?
Or is it that you thought, I deserved this?
As she cries out her anguish,
asking what she had done so wrong,
that it had cost her child life?
But as she slowly lifted up her head, she sees a rising mist.
She hears a whisper of something, of almost a tangible sound.
Yet something else, possibly?
And as she looks to see who it is, her eyes fall upon Him.
Standing only a few feet away.
There appears the image of a man with
a golden sword and a book.
He seems to be holding them, easily in his hands.
As slowly he approaches her, and speaking
softly, calming her with His soft words.
He stops beside her with a gentle smile and continues to speak.
I can hand you this Bible if you would so choose.
Or with this sword, I can do as you ask and take you now.
As you have begged me, this night to do.
But before you give me your answer,
on what you want me to do
with your life, please give me a moment of time.
I think first, you need to know a few things,
that may change your mind.
I have your precious child and he's here, at my side.
Then he paused to watch, as her grief-
stricken eyes lit up in surprise.
Then he continued, as if he knew what she needed to hear,
what she needed to know.
Oh, he is more than perfect, He said.
So much more, than you could ever have dreamed, him to be.

More than he could have ever been here, in this life.
But he's asked for me to tell you, that your
life has so much more worth.
For he never meant to live here, as an
ordinary child, not on this earth,
You haven't lost him.
It's just a visit delayed.
He paused for just a moment, as time
seemed to stand still for her,
as he patiently waited for her decision.
As if she alone would know her answer.
Looking up into His eyes,
she took an unsteady breath and wiped her tears
from her face. Shaking and trembling, she said,
"Lord, I'll take the Bible
if that's your will."
"But can you tell him that I love him,
and I'll keep him, in my heart,
as I have his pictures of him, upon my shelf?"
The Lord smiled
as he looked down so tenderly upon this heartbroken mother.
And He simply said, "Why don't you tell him for yourself?"
As from behind Him, her little boy stepped out,
with a cherubic smile upon his face, double dimples
showing just as she had imagined him to be.
She watched with all the love she had, more
than her heart could possibly contain.
With his blue eyes twinkling, under those
blonde tossed wisp of curls,
so softly falling over his brow.
There in that moment, as she saw him, he was exactly
as she had pictured him to be.
Oh, so many nights, in her dreams.
So, as she began to tell him of how she loved him.

From the very first moment she felt him move,
with all she had in her heart and soul.
She told him, all of her broken heart and dreams,
till she was spent and at last, she felt peace.
His twinkling eyes and his mischievous smile, said more
than he could have ever told her, in words.
As his love washed over her and softly
mending her broken heart.
And as he disappeared with a soft smile
and a wave to his mother,
he began rising through the mist.
She looked up to the heavens, watching to catch that last
glimpse of her baby boy, but they were nowhere to be found.
She felt a sharp pang of loss, mixed with her newfound peace,
but as she began to get up from her knees.
There lays a Lily upon the ground.
Lying there as if to let her know, he had been there all along.
A memento of a child's love,
for when he was gone.
She knew in that moment; it had not been a dream.
Although her heart was broken,
she knew in time her precious child, again she would see.
So, as she softly spoke his name and
touched the Lily to her lips.
She felt a peace wash over her, that only her God could give.
So now, in the early spring, as the Lily begins to bloom,
she remembers that sweet smile again.
Sees those twinkling, pretty blue eyes
with the dimples dipping in.
As he had looked when he smiled at her that day.
That thought, is and always will be comforting to her
each and every time, as she thinks back to that precious gift.
Just to know, that she will see him at her journeys end,
is enough for her to start her morning chores, with a smile now.
For now, as each new spring will begin again,

she will know peace upon the lilies bloom.
She will hear his laughter,
knowing he is watching her, with that smile.
As he sees her begin each day,
upon the Lily's bloom.

Laurie 2022

This Mirror of Time

A lifetime of past shadows, play in my mind.
Haunted memories of life.
Did I miss it?
Have I waited too long?
I see the shadows there, almost the same as yesterday's.
The same ones, as when I was young.
Those eyes, it's that smile that still haunts me.
Looking back at me, with the same unanswered questions.
The same, I had seen so many years ago,
looking back at me now,
in the reflection.
Of this mirror of time.

Laurie 2022

Moments Like Today

As I watched the vivid hues, of a fading
sunset dip below the horizon.
My heart feels as if it smiles, as I relax in quiet contentment.
My heart is full, and my soul is no longer at war, with the world.
As it is bathed in the quiet peacefulness, of the night.
The soft lull of the waves rolling softly over the sand,
creating ripples as the memories do the same,
In the back of my mind,
It's just one more reminder of the beautiful
moments, we can collect.
As I do the stones I find, as I walk along the Lake Shore.
As I stand still, leaning my head back watching the sky.
I am just amazed with the beauty of all around me,
as I smell the fresh air, coming in with the waves.
Taking in a deep breath and closing my eyes.
In that moment I feel the serenity of the quiet evening,
at its settles over me.
Like a warm and cozy blanket, I just settle in and relax.
This very moment is the reason why.
The very reason, I stopped looking for the next thing to buy.
The next place to go or the next person, to make me happy.
None of which, had ever really made me feel
alive or even passionate about anything, as if I
had ever had a true purpose in my life.
I thought having all of the latest and greatest,
would fill the empty places, but it never did.
I kept going from one place to the next, thinking I would find
what I was looking for.
Never once realizing, I was looking in all the wrong places,
for all of the wrong things.
Until I stopped one day and started listening to my own heart.
I stopped chasing the moments and the adventures.

I stopped finding new places, that I thought would make
me happy, or make me want to come alive again.
I had been wishing for something or someone, now I realize.
That would never have happened anywhere,
I had been looking.
But now, being present in my life, living in the moment.
Stepping back from the rush in life and appreciating the beauty
in the quiet moments of downtime.
This has changed everything about me and
what I thought, I wanted to find.
I want to do all the things in the world, that the
world seems to have forgotten about.
Lying in the sand under a star filled
sky, while off in the horizon,
the glow of the Northern Lights glow, as
they ribbon across the nights sky.
Turning down the noise of life and turning up the
music of nature. Feeling the wind in my hair.
Grasping at forever, as time passes through my hands.
That last song?
The last kiss.
At last bite of chocolate cake.
Those are the moments I will spend my life looking for.
For the contentment of just this moment in time.
Sure tomorrow, will still be there.
And reality, will always intrude.
It's always just around the corner.
I know that life will still be in motion, like a ship setting sail.
But today, right now, in this moment,
I want to immerse myself
in these immeasurable experiences that free my mind
Those moments, which electrify my spirit
in these moments, like today.
I could live forever.

Laurie 2022

How We Are

At this moment in time, right now.
There are so many all over the world,
who are just like you and me.
They're either lonely, scared or maybe just out of place.
Possibly missing someone or maybe just
wanting to go to that place,
they can call home.
They may be in love with someone, that they
probably shouldn't be in love with.
Or so they have been told.
They won't listen anyway, as humans never do.
Emotions hidden so deep inside; they
can't even escape from them.
Should they even try?
They can't even be seen.
They hide so deep, they wish for a quiet
moment, for just a moment.
For some Peace of Mind.
They dream of a better time, and they hope one day,
it will all go back to the way, it was before.
Before all the chaos of life began.
So, as they look out the window, whether in
the car, possibly on a bus or a train.
And do they watch people on the streets, wondering what
they have or if these people, have known the same pain?
Known the pain of uncertainty and indecisiveness, they
have ever felt this hopelessness in any time in their life.
They wonder if there are people out there
like them who feels this way.
Like they are just dancing in the wind?
But when they realize, they are like you and I
and you could tell them everything, that's going to happen,

and they still would never understand.
And right now, you're sitting here reading these words,
and I'm writing this for you and me, yet not for advice.
But so, we don't need to feel alone anymore, even though we
never take anyone's advice on how to change the chaos.
And we always have to find out for ourselves, the hard way.
Looking back some days and wishing I
had taken some of the wisdom
of my grandma's words to heart.
Maybe to have used for this time, in my life,
but being wise enough, knowing myself well enough,
to realize I would never have listened.
She already knew that.
That's just not how life works.
We live it, and then we try to understand.
Why no one ever takes that advice,
at that moment in time.

Laurie 2022

Where It Had Belonged

I sang myself to sleep tonight.
Beneath the ink black sky.
Thoughts of you still pierce through,
bringing with them to me, a smile.
Remembering the times we whiled away,
trading the hours for miles.
The lines on your face and reflective
hues of bright yellow and white.
Together we moved, with nothing to prove,
like soft shadows on the ground.
I fell into your waiting arms, as if a lost lover, I had found.
We talked and laughed, as the time flew past.
We danced and sang our songs.
My soul felt it was home, at last.
The only place
where it had belonged.

Laurie 2022

Printed in the United States
by Baker & Taylor Publisher Services